# IDENTITY

Joseph Shaules

Hiroko Tsujioka

Miyuki Iida

OXFORD
UNIVERSITY PRESS

# OXFORD
## UNIVERSITY PRESS

198 Madison Avenue
New York, NY 10016 USA

Great Clarendon Street
Oxford OX2 6DP England

Oxford New York

Auckland Bangkok Buenos Aires Cape Town Chennai
Dar es Salaam Delhi Hong Kong Istanbul Karachi Kolkata
Kuala Lumpur Madrid Melbourne Mexico City Mumbai
Nairobi São Paulo Shanghai Taipei Tokyo Toronto

OXFORD is a trademark of Oxford University Press.

ISBN 0-19-438574-4

Copyright © 2004 Oxford University Press

Editorial Manager: Nancy Leonhardt
Senior Editor: Chris Balderston
Editor: Patricia O'Neill
Associate Editors: Nishka Chandrasoma, Amy E. Hawley
Assistant Editor: Phebe W. Szatmari
Art Director: Lynn Luchetti
Design Project Manager: Maria Epes
Senior Designer: Claudia Carlson
Production Layout Artist: Elsa Varela
Art Editor: Judi DeSouter
Production Manager: Shanta Persaud
Production Coordinator: Eve Wong

Printing (last digit): 10 9 8 7 6 5 4 3

Printed in Hong Kong.

**Acknowledgments**

*Cover design:* Maria Epes
*Cover photo:* Kjeld Duits/JapaneseStreets.com
*Illustrations and realia by* Doron Ben-Ami, Janet Hamlin, Phillip
Howe/Deborah Wolfe, Ltd., Uldis Klavins, Vilma Ortiz Dillon

*The publishers would like to thank the following for their
permission to reproduce photographs:*
Gareth Brown/Corbis, Kathryn Sorrells, SuperStock, Jagdish
Agarwal/Alamy Images, John Foxx/Alamy Images, Image
100/Alamy Images, Liu Liqun/Corbis, Veer, Paul
Thompson/ImageState, Thomas F. Craig/IndexStock Imagery,
Image 100/Alamy Images, Kjeld Duits/JapaneseStreets.com,
courtesy of Kumiko Torikai, Ken Graham/AccentAlaska.com,
Yellow Dog Productions/Getty Images/The Image Bank, Corbis,
ASAP Ltd./IndexStock Imagery, IndexStock Imagery, C.
Borland/PhotoLink/PhotoDisc/PictureQuest, Kay
Chernush/United Media, Prisma/PSI/AGE Fotostock,
LWA-Dann Tardif/Corbis, Getty Images/PhotoDisc,
Larry Williams/Corbis, Getty Images, courtesy of the Institute
for Intercultural Studies, Inc., New York, LWA-Sharie
Kennedy/Corbis/SW Productions/IndexStock Imagery, Esbin-
Anderson/AGE Fotostock, James McLoughlin/AGE Fotostock,
Camelot/PPS Images, Stock Image/ImageState, Yong
He/ImagineChina, AP Worldwide Photos, Corbis, Michael
Paras/IndexStock Imagery, Hulton-Deutsch Collection/Corbis,
Douglas Peebles/Corbis

*The publishers would like to thank the following for their
permission to reproduce text:*

| | |
|---|---|
| p. 21 | Reprinted by permission of John Wiley & Sons, Inc. from *Gestures—The Do's and Taboos of Body Language Around the World* by Robert Axtell © John Wiley & Sons, Inc 1991 |
| p. 29 | PRINTED WITH PERMISSION FROM PSYCHOLOGY TODAY MAGAZINE, "Interview with Judith Martin (excerpt)" Copyright © (1998 Sussex Publishers, Inc.) |
| p. 33 | Reproduced with permission of The McGraw-Hill Companies, from *Riding the Waves of Culture 2nd Edition* by Fons Trompenaars, Alfons Trompenaars, and Charles Hampden Turner © The McGraw-Hill Companies 1997 |
| p. 41 | Reproduced by permission of Hal Glatzer, "What We Can Learn From Hawaii," by Hal Glatzer, copyright 1987 |
| p. 45 | Reproduced with permission from Little, Brown and Company from *Long Walk to Freedom* by Nelson Mandela © Little, Brown and Company 1994 |
| pp. 62–67 | Reproduced by permission of Oxford University Press from *The Advanced Learner's Dictionary of Current English 6th Edition* by A.S. Hornby © Oxford University Press 2000 |

*The publishers would like to acknowledge the following sources:*

| | |
|---|---|
| p. 5 | Hall, Edward. *Beyond Culture*. New York: Anchor Books, 1977 |
| p. 37 | Mead, Margaret. *Blackberry Winter: My Earlier Years*. New York: Kodansha International, 1995 |
| p. 49 | Gaston, Jan. *Cultural Awareness Teaching Techniques*. Brattleboro: Pro Lingua Associates, 1984 |

*The authors and publishers would like to thank the following
people for reviewing* Identity. *Their comments and suggestions
contributed to its development and helped shape its content.*
Atsuko Tsuda, David McMurray, Michael Furmanovsky,
Donna Fujimoto, Sarah Anne McAdam, Jeremie Roy,
Melissa Herbert, Elizabeth J. Lange, Ming-Yu Lee

*Special thanks to:*
Satoko Fukazawa
Charles Vilina
Satoko Shimoyama
Paul Riley
Julia Chang
Jung Ja Lee
Aki Ikeuchi

*Authors' acknowledgments:*
The authors would like to especially thank all the teachers of the
Cross-Cultural Communication Course at Rikkyo University for
their invaluable ideas, endless patience, and warm
encouragement. Additional thanks to the English Language
Program at Rikkyo, without whose official support this book
would not exist.

# TABLE OF CONTENTS

# LETTER TO STUDENT

Dear student,

Learning English will help you communicate with people from other countries. If you are simply traveling, the ability to have a basic conversation in English is enough. However, if you need to do business or live abroad, you will also need to have a deeper knowledge of the culture you are visiting.

*Identity* helps you do this by introducing you to ordinary people from around the world. They talk about their lives and give personal opinions about different cultural themes. *Identity* also introduces you to internationalists—cultural trainers, translators, political leaders, and teachers—so you can learn what experts say about culture and communication.

To communicate well with others, you need to have the confidence to use English to talk more deeply about yourself. *Identity* gives you this practice through discussion, presentation, and writing activities. You give opinions about what you've read, answer cultural questionnaires, talk about your experiences, and explain your culture. You will have the chance to express your ideas in your own way. So let your imagination run freely by using your own words and ideas to express your opinions about what is presented on the pages of this book.

We have enjoyed bringing together people from all over the world and putting them into this textbook. We hope you enjoy meeting them, and adding your voice to theirs.

**Joseph Shaules**

**Hiroko Tsujioka**

**Miyuki Iida**

# THEMES

Welcome to IDENTITY. Let's take a look at the design of the units.

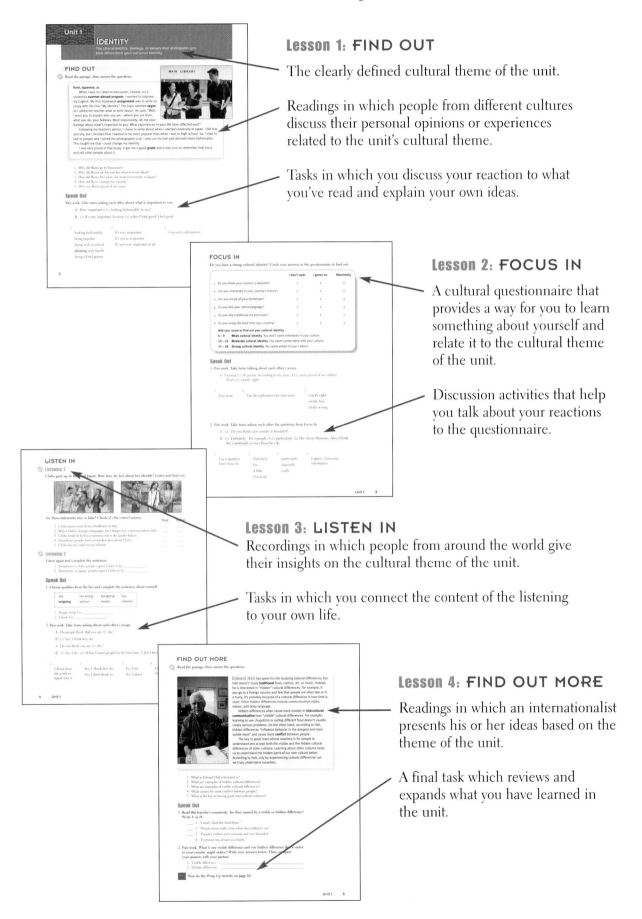

## Lesson 1: FIND OUT

The clearly defined cultural theme of the unit.

Readings in which people from different cultures discuss their personal opinions or experiences related to the unit's cultural theme.

Tasks in which you discuss your reaction to what you've read and explain your own ideas.

## Lesson 2: FOCUS IN

A cultural questionnaire that provides a way for you to learn something about yourself and relate it to the cultural theme of the unit.

Discussion activities that help you talk about your reactions to the questionnaire.

## Lesson 3: LISTEN IN

Recordings in which people from around the world give their insights on the cultural theme of the unit.

Tasks in which you connect the content of the listening to your own life.

## Lesson 4: FIND OUT MORE

Readings in which an internationalist presents his or her ideas based on the theme of the unit.

A final task which reviews and expands what you have learned in the unit.

# IDENTITY

The characteristics, feelings, or beliefs that distinguish you from others form your personal identity.

## FIND OUT

 Read the passage, then answer the questions.

MAIN LIBRARY

**Rumi, Japanese, 21**

When I was 20 I went to Vancouver, Canada, on a university **summer-abroad program**. I wanted to improve my English. My first homework **assignment** was to write an essay with the title "My Identity." The topic seemed **vague** so I asked the teacher what to write about. He said, "Well, I want you to explain who you are—where you are from, what you do, your hobbies. Most importantly, tell me your feelings about what's important to you. What experiences in your life have affected you?"

Following my teacher's advice, I chose to write about when I started university in Japan. I felt lost and shy, but I decided that I wanted to be more popular than when I was in high school. So, I tried to talk to people and I joined the photography club. I also cut my hair and dressed more fashionably. This taught me I could change my identity.

I was very proud of that essay. It got me a good **grade** and it was nice to remember that story and tell other people about it.

1. Why did Rumi go to Vancouver?
2. Why did Rumi ask her teacher what to write about?
3. How did Rumi feel when she started university in Japan?
4. How did Rumi change her identity?
5. Why was Rumi proud of her essay?

## Speak Out

**Pair work. Take turns asking each other about what is important to you.**

A: How important is (1) looking fashionable to you?

B: (2) It's very important because (3) when I look good, I feel good.

| 1 | 2 | 3 |
|---|---|---|
| looking fashionable | It's very important | *Give extra information.* |
| being popular | It's not so important | |
| doing well in school | It's not very important at all | |
| **pleasing** your family | | |
| being a kind person | | |

# FOCUS IN

Do you have a strong cultural identity? Circle your answers in the questionnaire to find out.

|  | I don't care! | I guess so. | Absolutely. |
|---|---|---|---|
| 1. Do you think your country is beautiful? | 1 | 2 | 3 |
| 2. Are you interested in your country's history? | 1 | 2 | 3 |
| 3. Are you proud of your hometown? | 1 | 2 | 3 |
| 4. Do you like your native language? | 1 | 2 | 3 |
| 5. Do you like traditional art and music? | 1 | 2 | 3 |
| 6. Do you enjoy the food from your country? | 1 | 2 | 3 |

**Add your score to find out your cultural identity.**

**6 – 9** **Weak cultural identity.** You don't seem interested in your culture.

**10 – 14** **Moderate cultural identity.** You seem comfortable with your culture.

**15 – 18** **Strong cultural identity.** You seem proud of your culture.

## Speak Out

1. Pair work. Take turns talking about each other's scores.

A: I scored (1) 16 points. According to my score, I (2) seem proud of my culture.
That's (3) exactly right.

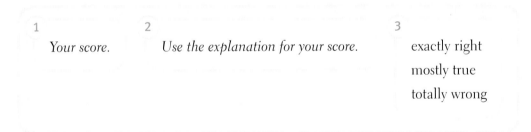

| 1 | 2 | 3 |
|---|---|---|
| *Your score.* | *Use the explanation for your score.* | exactly right<br>mostly true<br>totally wrong |

2. Pair work. Take turns asking each other the questions from Focus In.

A: (1) Do you think your country is beautiful?

B: (2) Definitely! For example, I (3) particularly (4) like cherry blossoms. Also, I think
the countryside is nicer than the city.

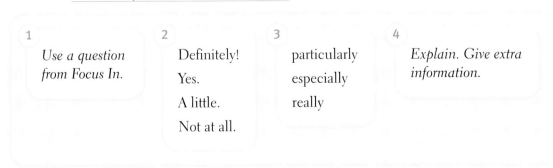

| 1 | 2 | 3 | 4 |
|---|---|---|---|
| *Use a question from Focus In.* | Definitely!<br>Yes.<br>A little.<br>Not at all. | particularly<br>especially<br>really | *Explain. Give extra information.* |

# LISTEN IN

Chiho grew up in Italy and Japan. How does she feel about her identity? Listen and find out.

Are these statements *true* or *false*? Check (✓) the correct answer.

|  | True | False |
|---|---|---|
| 1. Chiho spent most of her childhood in Italy. | ___ | ___ |
| 2. When Chiho changes languages, she changes her communication style. | ___ | ___ |
| 3. Chiho tends to be less expressive when she speaks Italian. | ___ | ___ |
| 4. Sometimes people have a mistaken idea about Chiho. | ___ | ___ |
| 5. Chiho has two sides to her identity. | ___ | ___ |

🔘 Listening 2

Listen again and complete the sentences.

1. Sometimes in Italy, people expect Chiho to be _____ .
2. Sometimes in Japan, people expect Chiho to be _____ .

## Speak Out

1. Choose qualities from the box and complete the sentences about yourself.

| | | | |
|---|---|---|---|
| shy | fun loving | easygoing | lazy |
| **outgoing** | serious | moody | cheerful |

1. People think I'm _____ .
2. I think I'm _____ .

2. Pair work. Take turns asking about each other's image.

A: Do people think that you are (1) shy?

B: (2) Yes, I think they do.

A: Do you think you are (1) shy?

B: (3) Yes, I do. (4) When I meet people for the first time, I don't know what to say.

| 1 | 2 | 3 | 4 |
|---|---|---|---|
| *Choose from the words in Speak Out 1.* | Yes, I think they do. No, I don't think so. | Yes, I do. No, I don't. | *Explain. Give extra information.* |

# FIND OUT MORE

Read the passage, then answer the questions.

**Edward Hall** has spent his life studying cultural differences, but Hall doesn't study **traditional** food, clothes, art, or music. Instead, he is interested in "hidden" cultural differences. For example, if you go to a foreign country and feel that people are often late or in a hurry, it's probably because of a cultural difference in how time is used. Other hidden differences include communication styles, values, and body language.

Hidden differences often cause more trouble in **intercultural communication** than "visible" cultural differences. For example, learning to use chopsticks or eating different food doesn't usually create serious problems. On the other hand, according to Hall, hidden differences "influence behavior in the deepest and most subtle ways" and cause more **conflict** between people.

The key to good intercultural relations is for people to understand and accept both the visible and the hidden cultural differences of other cultures. Learning about other cultures helps us to understand the hidden parts of our own culture better. According to Hall, only by experiencing cultural differences can we truly understand ourselves.

1. What is Edward Hall interested in?
2. What are examples of hidden cultural differences?
3. What are examples of visible cultural differences?
4. What causes the most conflict between people?
5. What is the key to having good intercultural relations?

## Speak Out

1. **Read this traveler's comments. Are they caused by a visible or hidden difference? Write *V* or *H*.**

   ____ 1. "I really liked the food there."

   ____ 2. "People stood really close when they talked to me."

   ____ 3. "People's clothes were unusual and very beautiful."

   ____ 4. "Everyone was always in a hurry."

2. **Pair work. What is one visible difference and one hidden difference that a visitor to your country might notice? Write your answers below. Then, compare your answers with your partner.**

   1. Visible difference: _____

   2. Hidden difference: _____

 **Now do the Wrap Up Activity on page 68.**

# VALUES

Values help us decide right and wrong, and guide us through difficult choices.

## FIND OUT

 Read the passage, then answer the questions.

> Kijana was in his second year at a university near London. One day he received a terrible phone call. He learned that his father was sick, so he immediately took a flight back to his hometown, Nairobi, Kenya. A week later he returned to England and made an announcement to his roommate, Matt.
>
> K: Matt, I'm afraid I have to go back to live in Kenya.
>
> M: What? You're going to quit school?
>
> K: My father had a heart attack. He's getting better, but the doctor told him that he can't work. I have to go back and help manage our family business.
>
> M: Your father ordered you to go back? Is that what you want?
>
> K: No, I don't like the family business. I'd rather study. Actually, my father said to stay here if I wanted, but some other relatives **insisted** I go back.
>
> M: Your relatives are being unfair! Don't **give in to** family pressure. You need to **stand up for** yourself.
>
> K: My biggest **responsibility** is to my family.
>
> M: I understand that your family is important to you, but you owe it to yourself to keep studying. You can't help your father by giving up your future.
>
> K: Thanks for caring, but I can't be **selfish** at a time like this.

1. Why did Kijana take a flight back to Kenya?
2. What announcement did Kijana make to his roommate?
3. What did Kijana's father tell him to do?
4. What advice does Matt give to Kijana?
5. Why does Kijana decide to go back to Kenya?

## Speak Out

**Pair work. Take turns asking questions about Kijana's situation and talking about your values.**

A: Do you think (1) he should go back to Kenya?

B: (2) No, I don't. I think it's important to (3) be independent. (4) I think he's old enough to decide things about his own life.

| 1 | 2 | 3 | 4 |
|---|---|---|---|
| he should go back to Kenya | Yes, I do. | be independent | *Explain. Give extra information.* |
| his relatives are being unfair | No, I don't. | respect your family's wishes | |
| it would be selfish for him to stay in London | | *Your idea:* | |

# FOCUS IN

What are your lifestyle values? Check (✓) your answers in the questionnaire.

| | | | |
|---|---|---|---|
| 1. Would you prefer to ... | lead an adventurous life? ☐ | lead a **stable** life? ☐ | not sure ☐ |
| 2. Do you prefer to ... | work for the future? ☐ | enjoy yourself now? ☐ | not sure ☐ |
| 3. Do you prefer to ... | ask for advice? ☐ | decide things for yourself? ☐ | not sure ☐ |
| 4. Do you prefer to do things ... | in groups? ☐ | alone? ☐ | not sure ☐ |
| 5. Would you prefer to ... | have a modern lifestyle? ☐ | have a traditional lifestyle? ☐ | not sure ☐ |

## Speak Out

**1. Pair work. Take turns discussing lifestyle values.**

A: (1) Would you prefer to lead an adventurous life or a stable life?

B: (2) I'd prefer to lead an adventurous life. (3) I like trying new things. I want to explore!
How about you?

| 1 | 2 | 3 |
|---|---|---|
| *Use a question from Focus In.* | *I'd prefer + your answer.*<br>I prefer + *your answer.*<br>I'm not sure. | *Explain. Give extra information.* |

**2. Pair work. Take turns asking about values in your country.**

A: Do you think (1) young people show respect for older people?

B: (2) No, I don't. For example, (3) they often do not give up their seats on trains for older people.

| 1 | 2 | 3 |
|---|---|---|
| young people show respect for older people<br>parents teach children to be independent<br>men and women have the same rights<br>education is very important<br>*Your idea:* _____ | Yes, I do.<br>No, I don't. | *Explain. Give extra information.* |

# LISTEN IN

## Listening 1

We learn many of our values from our family. Listen to Patricia, Ravi, and Nicole talk about the values they learned from their families.

**Patricia**

**Ravi**

**Nicole**

Which values do they talk about? Write *P*, *R*, or *N* next to the words.

| | | |
|---|---|---|
| _____ responsibility | _____ honesty | _____ respect |
| _____ **cooperation** | _____ keeping promises | _____ manners |

## Listening 2

Listen again. Who taught each person the values above?

Patricia: _____

Ravi: _____

Nicole: _____

## Speak Out

1. Every family has rules that help children learn values. What rules did your family have?

   | | |
   |---|---|
   | Manners: | "Don't talk with your mouth full." |
   | Effort: | "Always try to get good grades." |
   | Self-control: | "Do your homework before you watch TV." |
   | Respect: | "Do what your parents tell you." |
   | Your idea: | _____ |

   Read the examples below and add your own.

2. Value presentation. Prepare a presentation about how you learned values in your family. Answer the following questions.

   1. What rules are there in your family?
   2. What values did you learn from your family?
   3. What memories do you have about this?

   *Example:*

   1. In my family I was told, "Don't talk with your mouth full."
   2. I learned that manners are very important and I learned the value of politeness.
   3. I remember eating dinner with my family. Sometimes my mother said I was **messy**.

# FIND OUT MORE

 Read the passage, then answer the questions.

Masaki Yoshida teaches English at a cram school.

"I help students pass university entrance exams. I sometimes worry about them and their futures because they don't know what they want to study in college, or what kind of job they want in the future.

"A lot of my students go to college because their families expect them to. Many of them think that once they pass the entrance exam their future is **guaranteed**. That's a mistake. I tell them, 'Passing an entrance exam is just the beginning. To find a satisfying career you have to be able to answer the following questions: What do you want to learn about? What lifestyle do you want? What are your goals?'

"When I was younger, learning English and meeting people from other countries helped me think about my values and my future. I hope that my teaching can do the same for some of my students."

**"Passing an entrance exam is just the beginning."**

1. What is Masaki's job?
2. Why does Masaki worry about his students' future?
3. According to Masaki, why do many students go to college?
4. What mistake do many of his students make?
5. What helped Masaki think about his values?

## Speak Out

**Pair work. Take turns discussing your future.**

A: What do you want in the future?

B: I want (1) <u>challenging work.</u> (2) <u>I don't want a typical nine to five job. I get bored easily.</u>

A: What are your goals?

B: (3) <u>Within two years, I'd like to make enough money to buy a car.</u>

| 1 | 2 | 3 |
|---|---|---|
| challenging work | *Explain. Give extra information.* | *Your goal.* |
| a stable life | | |
| freedom | | |
| *Your idea:* _____ | | |

 **Now do the Wrap Up Activity on page 68.**

# CULTURE SHOCK

The stress people experience when they move to another culture.

## FIND OUT

 Read the passage, then answer the questions.

**Kenichi, Japanese, 21**

I spent my third year of high school in Orlando, Florida, on a study abroad program. I was excited when I first arrived. Later though, I became stressed because so much was new and **unfamiliar**. The food was different and I didn't have any friends. I couldn't **keep up with** conversations in English. Also, I needed to learn to **speak up** more. One day at a party the host offered me something to drink. I said, "No," even though I was thirsty. I thought he would insist, but he didn't. This taught me to say what I want. There were a lot of differences in communication like that.

After a month, I was really **depressed**. To try to get over culture shock, I decided to **get to know** my homestay family better and make at least one friend in school. Eventually, my English improved and I made several good friends. When I came back to Japan, I **stood out** because I had picked up certain habits from Americans, for example, how I dressed.

I'm glad I went to Florida because I learned that I could be **flexible** and **adapt**. If you go abroad, just remember that sometimes you might feel down, but things get easier as time goes by.

1. Why did Kenichi become stressed when he went to the United States?
2. What communication problems did he have?
3. What did he do to get over his culture shock?
4. What happened when he came back to Japan?
5. What did he learn about himself?

## Speak Out

1. What new things have you done in your life? Check (✓) your answers and add your own.

| | |
|---|---|
| ____ changed schools | ____ moved to a new neighborhood |
| ____ tried a new sport or hobby | ____ went to a foreign country |
| ____ joined a club or organization | Your idea: _____ |

2. Pair work. Take turns talking about new things you have done.

*Example:*

I changed schools when I was 12. I felt stressed at first because I had no friends. Eventually, I made friends and had a lot of fun.

# FOCUS IN

What personality type are you? Circle your answers in the questionnaire to find out.

|  | Definitely yes! | Maybe. | Maybe not. | Not at all. |
|---|---|---|---|---|
| 1. Do you often try new things or go to new places? | 1 | 2 | 3 | 4 |
| 2. Do you like meeting new people? | 1 | 2 | 3 | 4 |
| 3. Would you like to try living in a foreign country? | 1 | 2 | 3 | 4 |
| 4. Are you comfortable being alone? | 1 | 2 | 3 | 4 |
| 5. Do you like trying to speak a foreign language? | 1 | 2 | 3 | 4 |
| 6. Are you relaxed when you are with strangers? | 1 | 2 | 3 | 4 |

**Add your score to find out your personality type.**

**6 – 11** **Adventurous type.** You will probably adapt quickly to new environments.

**12 – 18** **Flexible type.** You will probably adapt with a little difficulty to new environments.

**19 – 24** **Careful type.** You may feel stress in a new environment. Try to learn about your new environment before you go.

## Speak Out

Pair work. Take turns asking about each other's personality type.

A: What's your personality type?

B: According to my score, I'm a (1) flexible type.

A: (2) Do you often try new things or go to new places?

B: (3) Yes! (4) I just went to Italy and Spain for the first time last year.

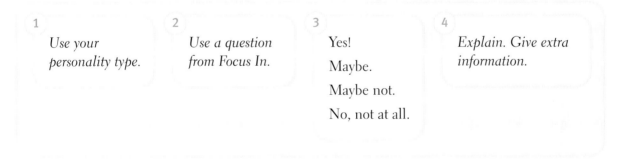

| 1 | 2 | 3 | 4 |
|---|---|---|---|
| *Use your personality type.* | *Use a question from Focus In.* | Yes! Maybe. Maybe not. No, not at all. | *Explain. Give extra information.* |

# LISTEN IN

## Listening 1

What two pieces of advice does Vincent give to people visiting Paris for the first time? Listen and check (✓) the advice.

____ what to do in the evenings
____ the best area to live
____ how to make friends
____ how to cook French food
____ where to shop

## Listening 2

Listen again. What specific advice does Vincent give? Write the answer.

1. What to do in the evenings: _____
2. Greetings: _____
3. Speaking French: _____

## Speak Out

Pair work. What advice would you give a person who has just moved to your neighborhood? Take turns asking the questions below.

1. Language: What words are useful to know?
2. Food: What food is good to try?
3. Friends: Where are good places to meet people?
4. Greeting customs: What greeting customs are useful to know?
5. Your idea: _____

*Giving Advice*

It's good to...
    You should...
        Why don't you...

*Examples:*

Language:  It is useful to know how to say hello. In Japanese, we say *konnichiwa* for hello.
Food:  You should try sushi. It is a very good traditional Japanese food.

# FIND OUT MORE

 Read the passage, then answer the questions.

Janet Bennett, an intercultural researcher and trainer, is an expert on culture shock. Her career started in 1968 when she experienced powerful culture shock as a **Peace Corps** volunteer in Micronesia. Janet and a group of other volunteers lived on separate islands. She says, "It was terrible because we didn't know culture shock existed. Everything was just the opposite from what we knew. All of us on our separate islands thought we were going crazy. Then we got together and found out that we were experiencing the same thing. Then someone mentioned the term culture shock."

According to Janet, the longer we stay abroad, the more different the culture, and the deeper our relationships with people, the greater the chance of having culture shock. Also, modern communication technology doesn't take away culture shock. Patience and flexibility are the keys to overcoming it. These days Janet does research and **intercultural training**. Learning to adapt to Micronesia started a learning process that continues even today.

1. Who is Janet Bennett?
2. When did she experience culture shock?
3. Why was culture shock terrible for Janet and the other volunteers?
4. What things increase the possibility of having culture shock?
5. What does she say are the keys to overcoming culture shock?

## Speak Out

Pair work. Read the questions below and write the answers. Take turns asking and answering the questions. Then share your answers with another pair.

You have a chance to visit a foreign country for a year.
1. Where will you go?
2. How will you prepare yourself before going?
3. What will you do when you are there?
4. Do you think you will have culture shock?
5. What will you do to reduce the culture shock after you have arrived?

 **Now do the Wrap Up Activity on page 69.**

# CULTURE IN LANGUAGE

Language and culture cannot be separated. A language reflects the culture of the people who speak it.

## FIND OUT

 Read the passage, then answer the questions.

**Mei-yeng, Chinese, 24**

In Chinese, the word for China consists of two Chinese characters. The first is "middle" and the second is "kingdom." China is a large country with an interesting past. The ancient Chinese thought that China was the center of the world. I like the feeling of this word because it reminds me of China's long history.

**Dale, American, 27**

In the United States you hear a lot of expressions using the word business, like "That's **none of your business**!" which means "That doesn't concern you." We also say "Let's get down to business," which means "Let's start working." These expressions are common because being successful in business is very important to us—though many people think hard work alone is more important. Americans always seem to be working!

**Michiko, Japanese, 18**

In Japanese, we have a special way to write words from foreign languages: *katakana*. Young people think it's cool to use these words. Sometimes my grandmother doesn't understand words I use like *toraburu*, meaning "to have trouble." I like the sound of words like that because they show the flexibility of the Japanese. Japanese people like new things so we borrow a lot of words.

1. What did the ancient Chinese think about China?
2. Why does Mei-yeng like this word?
3. Why are business expressions common in the United States?
4. What do many Americans find even more important than being successful in business?
5. What do young Japanese think about foreign words?

## Speak Out

Pair work. Take turns talking about your language.

A: How do you feel about (1) Japanese? Do you think it (2) expresses Japanese culture?

B: (3) Yes. (4) It has a lot of formal language. Being polite is important in Japan.

| 1 | 2 | 3 | 4 |
|---|---|---|---|
| *Your language.* | expresses (*your country's*) culture<br>has many interesting words<br>is difficult to learn | Yes.<br>Not really.<br>I'm not sure. | *Explain. Give extra information.* |

# FOCUS IN

Do you agree with the proverbs below? Read, then check (✓) your answer.

|  |  |  | I agree. | I disagree. |
|---|---|---|---|---|
| 1. | Proverb: | The **squeaky** wheel gets the grease. | ____ | ____ |
|  | Advice: | You should speak up to get what you want. | ____ | ____ |
| 2. | Proverb: | Good fences make good neighbors. | ____ | ____ |
|  | Advice: | To get along with people, you shouldn't try to get too close! | ____ | ____ |
| 3. | Proverb: | Nothing **ventured**, nothing gained. | ____ | ____ |
|  | Advice: | It's good to take chances. | ____ | ____ |
| 4. | Proverb: | God helps those that help themselves. | ____ | ____ |
|  | Advice: | You should do things yourself and not depend on others for help. | ____ | ____ |

## Speak Out

1. Pair work. Take turns asking each other about the proverbs in Focus In.

> A:  Do you think (1) you should speak up to get what you want?
>
> B:  I think that's (2) great advice. (3) Many people don't say what they want clearly. If you say what you want, you will get what you want.

| 1 | 2 | 3 |
|---|---|---|
| *Use the advice in Focus In.* | great advice <br> often true <br> sometimes true <br> terrible advice | *Explain. Give extra information.* |

2. Group work. In groups, think of the advice of a proverb that you agree with. Then share your information with another group.

> *Example:*
>
> Proverb:  *Ishibashi wo tataite wataru.* (Japanese)
> Translation:  Knock on the stone bridge before crossing.
> Meaning:  Check carefully before starting something new.
> We agree because things are not always what they seem.

# LISTEN IN

Every language has expressions or idioms. English has many of them. Listen to Robert and Yoshi's conversation. Write the numbers 1–4 next to the idioms in the order you hear them.

_____ It sounded fishy.

_____ I blew my top.

_____ I'm crazy about her.

_____ Keep it under your hat.

Listen again and draw lines to match the idioms with their meanings.

| | |
|---|---|
| 1. It sounded fishy. | A. Don't tell anyone about this. |
| 2. I blew my top. | B. I didn't think he was telling me the truth. |
| 3. I'm crazy about her. | C. I started yelling at him. |
| 4. Keep it under your hat. | D. I really love her. |

## Speak Out

1. Here are four more idioms in English. Write *H* next to the idioms used when someone is happy and *A* next to the idioms used when someone is angry.
   Check your answers with another student.

   _____ I was on cloud nine.

   _____ I freaked out.

   _____ I lost my cool.

   _____ I felt ten feet tall.

2. Pair work. In your native language, write down two words, phrases, or idioms that express the following emotions: happiness and anger. Share your answers with two other people.

   _____    _____

   _____    _____

# FIND OUT MORE

Read the passage, then answer the questions.

Kumiko Torikai is a translation and language education expert. According to her, careers that use English also require cultural skills. For example, "to be a good translator you must understand two cultures, not just two languages." One reason is that some words are difficult to translate, such as the word *hansei* in Japanese. "In English we can say **'reflect on'** or 'feel **remorse**.' But neither is quite right because *hansei* is closely connected to Japanese culture and it's a challenge to express it in English."

Other jobs also require cultural skills. Language teachers must teach not only words and grammar, but also cultural background and conversational style. International business people must often adapt their working style or sales techniques to the cultural expectations of other countries. People who work with the public, such as tour guides, hotel workers, and flight attendants, need to be outgoing and also understand the customs and manners of their guests or customers. In fact, according to Ms. Torikai, "Every job which uses a foreign language requires cultural knowledge and skills."

So what's Ms. Torikai's advice for people interested in international work? "To be a successful professional you need language skills, but also a **genuine** interest in people and their culture. Put these two things together and you can have a great career."

1. What is needed to be a good translator?
2. Why is *hansei* difficult to express in English?
3. What do language teachers need to teach?
4. What do people who work with the public need to understand?
5. What two things are needed to have an international career?

## Speak Out

**Pair work. Take turns discussing the challenges of international careers.**

A: Do you think working as a (1) <u>tour guide</u> would be hard?

B: Well, you need (2) <u>to be outgoing.</u> (3) <u>I think it would be fun, but maybe I would get bored after a while.</u>

| 1 | 2 | 3 |
|---|---|---|
| A *career mentioned in the reading, or your own idea.* | to be outgoing<br>great language skills<br>to know customs and manners<br>to adapt to other cultures | *Talk about whether you would like this job.* |

Now do the Wrap Up Activity on page 69.

# BODY LANGUAGE AND CUSTOMS

Every culture has customs that are related to body language,
or nonverbal communication.

## FIND OUT

 Read the passage, then answer the questions.

**Lyn, Chinese, 22**
    When I studied in California, I was surprised to see couples kissing in
public, like on a bench on campus, and holding hands when they walked.
I was also often **hugged** by my good American friends. Where I come
from in China, these things aren't common. I was **embarrassed** at first.
I learned that people from other cultures use very different body
language to express their feelings.

**Bill, American, 35**
    When I worked in Saudi Arabia, I often saw male friends holding hands.
Once a Saudi friend took my hand as he showed me the way into his house.
Also, I felt that people stood very close to each other when they talked. At first
I was surprised and sometimes felt a little uncomfortable. I learned how
powerful body language really is.

1. What body language was Lyn surprised to see?
2. How did she feel about being hugged?
3. What did Lyn learn about body language?
4. What body language did Bill often see in Saudi Arabia?
5. How did Saudi body language make Bill feel at first?

## Speak Out

**Pair work. Take turns asking each other about body language you have seen.**

A: Have you ever seen (1) couples kissing in public?

B: (2) Yes, I have. (3) But not a lot. When I was in America, I saw many more couples
kissing than here.

| 1 | 2 | 3 |
|---|---|---|
| couples kissing in public<br>people standing close when talking<br>good friends hugging each other<br>people bowing to show respect<br>*Your idea:* _____ | Yes, I have.<br>No, I haven't. | *Explain. Give extra information.* |

# FOCUS IN

Read these statements about customs in different countries. Did you know about these customs? Check (✓) your answers.

|  | I knew that. | I didn't know that. |
|---|---|---|
| 1. It's rude to touch a child on the head. (Thailand) | ____ | ____ |
| 2. Men and women rarely touch in public. (Saudi Arabia) | ____ | ____ |
| 3. It's rude for the bottom of your feet to point at someone. (Malaysia) | ____ | ____ |
| 4. Eating with your fingers is common. (Egypt) | ____ | ____ |
| 5. Hugging is a common greeting. (the United States) | ____ | ____ |
| 6. People sometimes point using their lips. (Philippines) | ____ | ____ |
| 7. People often kiss each other on the cheek. (Italy) | ____ | ____ |

## Speak Out

1. Pair work. Take turns discussing the customs in Focus In.

> A: I've heard that in (1) Thailand, it's rude to touch a child on the head. Did you know that?
>
> B: (2) Yes, I did. In (3) Japan, that's not true. It's OK to touch children on the head.

| 1 | 2 | 3 |
|---|---|---|
| *Use a statement from Focus In.* | Yes, I did. <br> No, I didn't. | *Give information about body language and customs in your country.* |

2. Group work. List four habits that are rude in your country. Share your list with another group.

*Example:*

In Korea, it is rude to blow your nose in public.

1. _____
2. _____
3. _____
4. _____

# LISTEN IN

Listen to Jerzy, Leena, and Stephanie talk about customs in Poland, India, and Greece. Circle the correct information.

1. In Poland, it's important to bring an  even number / odd number  of flowers to someone's house.
2. In Poland, greeting each person individually is considered impolite / polite.
3. In India, *namaste* can be used to say hello or good-bye / hello.
4. Dinner parties in Greece have no set ending time / last only two hours.
5. In Greece, it's impolite / acceptable to interrupt other people when they're talking.

## Listening 2

Listen again and answer the questions.

1. In Poland, how should people greet one another? _____
2. In India, what is the gesture of *namaste*? _____
3. In Greece, why isn't it important to arrive exactly on time? _____

## Speak Out

1. Pair work. Take turns describing customs in your country.

A: In (Japan), do people generally (1) greet each other with a kiss?

B: (2) No, they don't. (3) In (Japan), people bow when they greet each other.

| 1 | 2 | 3 |
|---|---|---|
| bow | No, they don't. | *Explain. Give extra information.* |
| hug when they meet a friend | Yes, they do. | |
| greet each other with a kiss | Sometimes. | |
| bring gifts or flowers when they go to someone's house | | |
| walk arm in arm as a couple | | |

# FIND OUT MORE

 Read the passage, then answer the questions.

Kissing is found in all cultures. Though it's common, there's a lot of cultural variation. Among the Tapuya of South America only men kiss— it's a sign of peace. In the Philippines, vendors in the market sometimes use a kissing sound to attract customers. In many countries, people kiss as a greeting. While the French and Italians kiss the air next to the cheek, Russians actually kiss the other person's cheek.

Of course kissing is also for couples. According to research, eight percent of kissers in the United States keep their eyes open, and twenty percent sometimes look. In English, people say "French kiss" to mean a deep, passionate kiss, but the French don't have a special word for this.

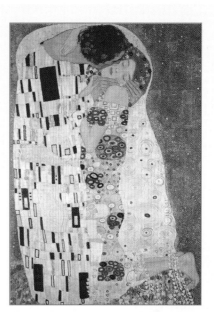

Kissing can also be found in art. Two famous examples are Rodin's statue and Klimt's painting, both called *The Kiss*. Hollywood has given us kissing scenes in thousands of movies, while in India it's not permitted on the screen. Kissing is everywhere, but when and how depends on culture!

1. What does kissing mean to the Tapuya of South America?
2. Why do Filipino vendors sometimes make a kissing sound?
3. What's the difference between the Russian and French greeting kiss?
4. In what works of art can we find kissing?
5. In what country is kissing not permitted in movies?

## Speak Out

**Pair work. Take turns talking about kissing.**

A: How do you feel about (1) using a kissing sound to attract customers?

B: I think it's a/an (2) odd custom. I tend to be (3) curious about things like that. (4) I wonder where that custom came from.

| 1 | 2 | 3 | 4 |
|---|---|---|---|
| using a kissing sound to attract customers | interesting | easygoing | *Explain. Give extra information.* |
| | **odd** | uncomfortable | |
| kissing as a sign of peace | **cool** | shy | |
| kissing on the lips as a greeting | shocking | curious | |

 **Now do the Wrap Up Activity on page 70.**

# Unit 6

# INDIVIDUALISM

People who value individualism feel that it's important to be independent and do things on one's own.

## FIND OUT

 Read the passage, then answer the questions.

**David, Israeli, 19**

Individualism brings out the best in people. If we always have to follow social rules and worry about what others think, there's no way we can be happy because we can't be ourselves. People need freedom to be creative and for society to be dynamic. In my case, if I need help from my friends, I'll ask. They would never tell me what to do. I'm the person responsible for me and my life.

**Rosa, Portuguese, 21**

I prefer doing things with my friends and family rather than alone. I don't understand people who are always trying to be different from everyone else. I think too much individualism hurts society because it makes people selfish. It's important to care for the people around us and be responsible for others. I think it's good for people to depend on each other.

1. What does David think brings out the best in people?
2. According to David, what will happen if we always have to follow social rules?
3. What would David's friends never do to him?
4. What does Rosa think too much individualism does?
5. According to Rosa, what is important?

## Speak Out

**Pair work. Take turns discussing what Rosa and David say.**

A: Do you agree with (1) Rosa when he/she says that (2) too much individualism makes people selfish?

B: (3) Absolutely. (4) If everyone just thinks about themselves, they will forget to be kind.

| 1 | 2 | 3 | 4 |
|---|---|---|---|
| Rosa David | too much individualism makes people selfish | Absolutely. | *Explain. Give extra information.* |
| | people need freedom to be creative | Somewhat. | |
| | we need to be responsible for others | Not really. | |

# FOCUS IN

Are you an individualist or a **collectivist**? Circle the numbers that correspond to your answers in the questionnaire and find out.

|  | Yes. | Usually. | Sometimes. | No. |
|---|---|---|---|---|
| 1. Do you enjoy being different? | 1 | 2 | 3 | 4 |
| 2. Do you check with others before making decisions? | 4 | 3 | 2 | 1 |
| 3. Do you prefer to work or study by yourself? | 1 | 2 | 3 | 4 |
| 4. Do you have more fun in groups? | 4 | 3 | 2 | 1 |
| 5. Do you prefer **one-on-one** friendships? | 1 | 2 | 3 | 4 |
| 6. Do you feel comfortable following others? | 4 | 3 | 2 | 1 |

**Add your score.**

| 6 – 10 | **Strong individualist.** |
|---|---|
| 11 – 15 | **Individualist.** |
| 16 – 19 | **Collectivist.** |
| 20 – 24 | **Strong collectivist.** |

## Speak Out

Pair work. Take turns talking about each other's results.

A: What's your score?

B: It's (1) 14. According to the result, I'm a/an (2) individualist.

A: (3) Do you enjoy being different?

B: (4) Sometimes. (5) For example, I like having an unusual haircut.

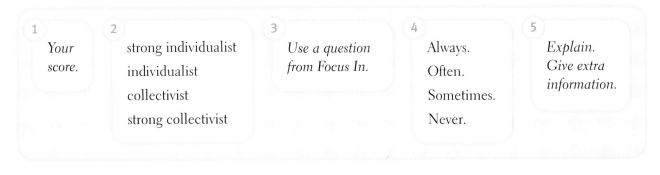

| 1 | 2 | 3 | 4 | 5 |
|---|---|---|---|---|
| *Your score.* | strong individualist<br>individualist<br>collectivist<br>strong collectivist | *Use a question from Focus In.* | Always.<br>Often.<br>Sometimes.<br>Never. | *Explain. Give extra information.* |

# LISTEN IN

Listen to Naoko and Ahmed talk about what groups are important where they live.
Check (✓) the groups that are mentioned.

| ____ family | ____ co-workers | ____ people from your neighborhood |
|---|---|---|
| ____ religious groups | ____ **ethnic** groups | ____ friends from school |

## Listening 2

Listen again and answer the questions.

1. Why does Naoko think it's good to go out with people from work? _____
2. Why does Ahmed think that family relationships are valuable? _____

## Speak Out

**Pair work. Take turns talking about the people you spend time with.**

A: Do you enjoy spending time in groups?

B: I like to do things (1) in groups  because (2) things are livelier.

A: What do you do with (3) friends from school?

B: (4) I often go out to eat with them after class. We talk about everything. It's a lot of fun.

| 1 | 2 | 3 | 4 |
|---|---|---|---|
| one-on-one | things are livelier | friends from school | *Explain. Give extra information.* |
| in groups | you can get to know each other better | family | |
| | *Your idea:* | *Your idea:* | |
| | | | |

# FIND OUT MORE

 Read the passage, then answer the questions.

**Steve MacAllister,** a cross-cultural trainer, helps prepare Americans who are going to work in foreign countries. According to Steve, "One challenge for many Americans is learning to work in companies or countries with more collectivist working styles."

In some companies, each person tends to be given clear and separate responsibilities. In others, people tend to work together and share responsibility and **credit**. According to Steve, "If the manager and the employees have different working styles, it often leads to problems." An American manager may feel that collectivist employees avoid responsibility. On the other hand, a collectivist manager may feel that individualist employees are **uncooperative**.

"Neither style is better, just different," says Steve. However, managers and employees from different cultures need to understand both working styles.

*Working styles in different countries.*

Q: In your company, what kind of working style is more common?
   a. People work together, and you do not get individual credit. (collectivist answer)
   b. People are allowed to work individually, and individual credit can be received. (individualist answer)

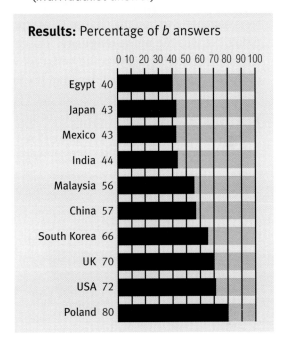

**Results:** Percentage of *b* answers

| Country | Percentage |
|---------|-----------|
| Egypt | 40 |
| Japan | 43 |
| Mexico | 43 |
| India | 44 |
| Malaysia | 56 |
| China | 57 |
| South Korea | 66 |
| UK | 70 |
| USA | 72 |
| Poland | 80 |

1. What is Steve MacAllister's job?
2. What is one challenge for Americans working in other countries?
3. What happens if managers and employees have different working styles?
4. How might an American manager feel about collectivist employees?
5. How might a collectivist manager feel about individualist employees?

## Speak Out

Pair work. An American is coming to work in your country. What might be difficult for him or her? Together, write four things below. Then, share your answers with another pair.

1. _____
2. _____
3. _____
4. _____

 Now do the Wrap Up Activity on page 70.

# POLITENESS

The way people treat each other in order to show courtesy and respect.

## FIND OUT

 Read the passage, then answer the questions.

**Josh, American, 21**

I've been studying Japanese at a university in Oregon. Last year, I went to Tokyo for a seminar and had the chance to practice the Japanese I had learned. One thing I didn't like was the **polite language.** It seemed so cold. Everybody called me by my last name. Students used polite language with me, and very polite language with the professor. I think respect comes from the heart, not from one's age or status. When I used **formal** language to talk to people, I felt distant from them.

**Young-hee, Korean, 22**

When I first started studying at UCLA, I was surprised at how informal students were. Some sat very **casually** at their desks and sometimes brought drinks into the lectures. They even openly disagreed with the professors. On campus, students casually greeted professors by saying "Hi," and walking away. I understand that's because Americans try to treat everyone equally. But to me it seems rude. I think it's important to show extra courtesy to the people we respect.

1. How did Josh feel about Japanese polite language?
2. What does Josh think about respect?
3. What was Young-hee surprised at?
4. According to Young-hee, why do Americans greet professors casually?
5. What is important for Young-hee?

## Speak Out

**Pair work. Take turns talking about politeness in the classroom.**

A: Do you think that (1) using informal language with teachers is impolite?

B: (2) It depends. (3) In Japan, students sometimes use informal language with young teachers.

| 1 | 2 | 3 |
|---|---|---|
| using informal language with teachers | Absolutely. | *Explain how things are in your country.* |
| sitting casually in class | It depends. | |
| disagreeing with teachers | Not at all. | |
| bringing a drink into the classroom | | |

# FOCUS IN

Are you a formal or casual person? Compare yourself with Mr. Casual and find out.

|  | I agree. | It depends. | I disagree. |
|---|---|---|---|
| 1. Mr. Casual thinks we should use first names with everyone. | 1 | 2 | 3 |
| 2. Mr. Casual thinks wearing formal clothes is boring. | 1 | 2 | 3 |
| 3. Mr. Casual thinks we shouldn't treat each other differently because of age. | 1 | 2 | 3 |
| 4. Mr. Casual thinks we should stop using formal language. | 1 | 2 | 3 |
| 5. Mr. Casual thinks casual people are friendlier. | 1 | 2 | 3 |
| 6. Mr. Casual thinks everyone should treat each other equally. | 1 | 2 | 3 |

**Add your score to find out if you are formal or casual.**
**6 – 9      You are super-casual.**
**10 – 13   You are semi-casual.**
**14 – 18   You are formal.**

Mr. Casual

## Speak Out

1. Pair work. Take turns talking about each other's scores.

   A: What's your result?

   B: According to my score, I'm (1) super-casual. (2) In fact, all my friends are super-casual, too.

   | 1 | 2 |
   |---|---|
   | *Your result.* | *Explain. Give extra information.* |

2. Pair work. Take turns discussing Mr. Casual's ideas.

   A: (1) Mr. Casual thinks we should use first names with everyone. Do you agree?

   B: (2) No, I don't. (3) It would be weird to call my parents by their first names.

   | 1 | 2 | 3 |
   |---|---|---|
   | *Use a statement from Focus In.* | No, I don't. Yes, I do. | *Explain. Give extra information.* |

# LISTEN IN

Listen to Mohamed and Cameron talk about a person they respect. Write *M* for Mohamed or *C* for Cameron next to the items they mention.

____ look him in the eye      ____ don't call him by his first name

____ **bow** politely      ____ stand up when a teacher enters the room

____ stop talking      ____ listen to what he says

## Listening 2

Listen again and answer the following questions.

1. Why did Mohamed respect his science teacher? _____

2. What is Cameron's father's personality like? _____

## Speak Out

Pair work. Write a description about a person you respect. Complete the following sentences. Then, tell your partner about this person.

1. Introduction: Let me tell you about _____

2. Description: He/She is _____

3. Reasons for respect: I respect him/her because _____

4. Showing respect: I show my respect by _____

5. Extra information: _____ _____

6. Ending: In conclusion, _____

*Helpful Words*

| | | |
|---|---|---|
| hardworking | passionate | caring |
| responsible | easygoing | helpful |

*Example:*

*Let me tell you about* my mother. *She is* 44 years old, and she's very hardworking. She has a job, but she also takes care of me and my sister. *I respect her because* she's busy but makes time to have fun with us. *I show my respect by* doing what she asks me to do, and helping her. My mother loves plants, so I help her by watering them after school. *In conclusion,* I think we should appreciate the things our parents do for us.

# FIND OUT MORE

Read the passage, then answer the questions.

Judith Martin is an American who cares about social skills. She became interested in **etiquette** when she was a reporter for the Washington Post. She now writes a well-known newspaper column, "Miss Manners," in which she gives advice on etiquette.

Ms. Martin believes that etiquette is not simply about being polite, it's about communication. "People think, mistakenly, that etiquette means you have to **suppress** your differences. On the contrary, etiquette is what enables you to deal with them; it gives you a set of rules," she says. "Of course, these rules for polite behavior depend on culture."

One obvious area of cultural difference is manners during meals. In some countries, you pray before eating. In the Arab world, you eat with your fingers, but never use the left hand. In most of Asia, you shouldn't stand chopsticks up in rice. In China you often leave a bit of food on your plate, while in the United States you eat everything. As Ms. Martin teaches us, learning etiquette shows respect for the customs of other cultures, and can be a first step in good intercultural relationships.

1. When did Judith Martin become interested in etiquette?
2. What does Ms. Martin do in her column "Miss Manners"?
3. What does she believe about etiquette?
4. What obvious area of cultural difference in etiquette is mentioned in the passage?
5. Why should we learn the etiquette of other cultures?

## Speak Out

**Pair work. Take turns discussing the customs mentioned in the reading.**

A: (1) In some countries, people pray before eating. Did you know that?

B: (2) Yes, I knew that. That seems quite (3) interesting to me. (4) In Japan, we say something before we eat, but we don't pray.

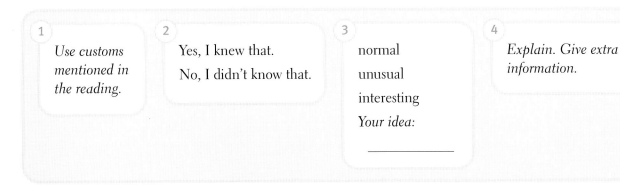

| 1 | 2 | 3 | 4 |
|---|---|---|---|
| *Use customs mentioned in the reading.* | Yes, I knew that.<br>No, I didn't know that. | normal<br>unusual<br>interesting<br>*Your idea:*<br>_____ | *Explain. Give extra information.* |

**Now do the Wrap Up Activity on page 70.**

# COMMUNICATION STYLES

The different ways in which people express themselves.

## FIND OUT

 Read the passage, then answer the questions.

**Esteban, Spanish, 26**

We met at university in London. I tend to be **expressive**—I mean, if I feel something, I show it openly. After a few dates with Mulatu I was very direct and told her I was in love with her, but she seemed very **reserved**. When I asked her, "Don't you love me?" she said, "Of course I do. You didn't notice?" The difference in our communication styles sometimes leads to arguments. Once she was angry at me for two days but I didn't realize it because she didn't say so directly. If she's **upset**, I want her to tell me immediately!

**Mulatu, Ethiopian, 27**

I first saw Esteban in my economics class. I was totally in love with him from the beginning and I was surprised that he didn't notice how I felt. I guess he wanted me to say something directly, but if you love someone I think words shouldn't be necessary. Esteban isn't **subtle**, and our communication gap is frustrating sometimes. When something bothers him, he gets very **emotional**. I wish he'd change— that he would be calmer.

1. What leads to arguments in Esteban and Mulatu's relationship?
2. What does Esteban want Mulatu to do if she's upset?
3. Why didn't Mulatu tell Esteban directly that she loved him?
4. How does Mulatu feel about the communication gap between her and Esteban?
5. How would Mulatu like Esteban to change?

## Speak Out

**Pair work. Take turns asking about the kinds of people you communicate well with.**

A: Do you get along well with people who are (1) expressive?

B: (2) Yes, I do. (3) My friends show their feelings openly. Our conversations are pretty wild sometimes!

| 1 | | 2 | 3 |
|---|---|---|---|
| expressive | reserved | Yes, I do. | *Explain. Give extra information.* |
| direct | loud | No, I don't. | |
| calm | | | |

# FOCUS IN

What kind of communication style do you have? Circle your answers in the questionnaire to find out.

1. If a friend is angry with you, do you:
   a. discuss the problem immediately?
   b. wait until later to discuss it?

2. With your best friend, do you:
   a. talk a lot with each other?
   b. understand each other without words?

3. When you're very excited, do you:
   a. express your feelings openly?
   b. act calmly and keep your feelings inside?

4. When you make a new friend, do you:
   a. talk openly about yourself?
   b. take time before talking openly?

5. In a romantic relationship, is it more important to:
   a. be honest?
   b. be sensitive?

6. To avoid misunderstandings, is it more important to:
   a. explain yourself clearly?
   b. notice the feelings of others?

**Add your score to find out what kind of communication style you have. (a = 1 point / b = 2 points)**

**6 – 7    You have an expressive communication style.**

**8 – 10   You have a flexible communication style.**

**11 – 12  You have a reserved communication style.**

## Speak Out

Pair work. Take turns talking about each other's communication styles.

A: What's your communication style?

B: According to the questionnaire, I have (1) a reserved communication style.

A: So, (2) if a friend is angry with you, do you prefer to discuss the problem immediately or wait until later?

B: (3) I prefer to wait until later. (4) I think you should be calm when you discuss something.

| 1 | 2 | 3 | 4 |
|---|---|---|---|
| *Your result.* | *Use a question from Focus In.* | *Your answer from Focus In.* | *Explain. Give extra information.* |

# LISTEN IN

Listen to John and Keiko talk about different communication styles in the workplace. Are the statements *true* or *false*? Check (✓) the correct answer.

|   |   | True | False |
|---|---|---|---|
| 1. | Keiko was a new employee at the company. | ____ | ____ |
| 2. | John is older than Keiko. | ____ | ____ |
| 3. | Keiko noticed that John was making mistakes. | ____ | ____ |
| 4. | Keiko mentioned John's mistakes to him directly. | ____ | ____ |
| 5. | John felt that Keiko talked behind his back. | ____ | ____ |

## Listening 2

Listen again and answer the questions.

1. What kind of communication does John like? _____

2. What does Keiko wish that John understood? _____

## Speak Out

**1. Pair work. Take turns giving advice.**

A: I've got a problem. (1) My colleague is not doing a good job.

B: That's too bad. (2) I think you should (3) talk to your **colleague** directly. Perhaps you can ask him/her if he/she needs help.

| 1 | 2 | 3 |
|---|---|---|
| My colleague is not doing a good job. | I think you should | *Give advice.* |
| My best friend did something that hurt my feelings. | Why don't you | |
| My sister fell in love, but I think she's making a mistake. | | |

**2. Pair work. What's the best advice for these situations? Discuss with your partner and write your answers. Then share them with another pair.**

1. My boyfriend/girlfriend lied to me. _____

2. I think my sister stole some money. _____

3. My parents want me to work in the family business, but I don't want to. _____

_____

# FIND OUT MORE

Read the passage, then answer the questions.

Fons Trompenaars gives training to international managers. According to Fons, people who come from countries with emotionally **neutral** cultures tend to keep their feelings controlled, while people from countries with more emotionally expressive cultures show their feelings **plainly**, by raising their voices, laughing, gesturing, etc. In international business that can sometimes cause problems.

According to Mr. Trompenaars, people from emotionally neutral cultures often think that showing a lot of emotion at work is "unprofessional." On the other hand, people from an emotionally expressive culture may find neutral colleagues to be "cold" or "unfeeling." Neither of these stereotypes is true. People from all cultures have the same feelings, but how the feelings are expressed is different.

Mr. Trompenaars has collected data on cultural difference. The following question comes from research that tries to find out which countries tend more toward being expressive or neutral.

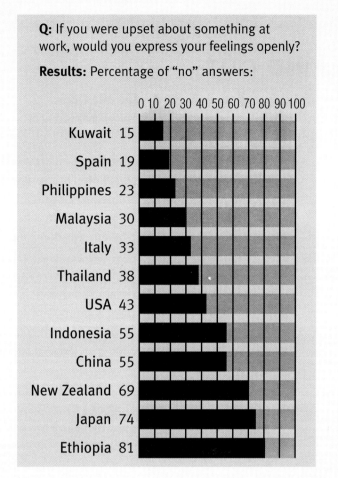

**Q:** If you were upset about something at work, would you express your feelings openly?

**Results:** Percentage of "no" answers:

| Country | % |
|---|---|
| Kuwait | 15 |
| Spain | 19 |
| Philippines | 23 |
| Malaysia | 30 |
| Italy | 33 |
| Thailand | 38 |
| USA | 43 |
| Indonesia | 55 |
| China | 55 |
| New Zealand | 69 |
| Japan | 74 |
| Ethiopia | 81 |

1. What does Fons Trompenaars do?
2. How do people from emotionally expressive cultures show their feelings?
3. What do people from emotionally neutral cultures think about showing emotion at work?
4. How might business people from emotionally expressive cultures feel about emotionally neutral colleagues?
5. What does Mr. Trompenaars' research try to find out?

## Speak Out

Prepare a presentation about your country. Answer the following questions.

1. Is the communication style in your culture expressive or neutral?
2. How do people show feelings in your country?
3. What kind of communication style do you like?

*Example:*

In Korea, the communication style is expressive. People laugh out loud when something is funny and raise their voices when they get excited. If you care about something, you should show your feelings. I like warm and friendly communication.

 Now do the Wrap Up Activity on page 71.

# GENDER AND CULTURE

Every culture has different expectations about gender roles
and the communication styles of men and women.

## FIND OUT

 Read the passage, then answer the questions.

**Eun-suk, Korean, 28**

Traditionally in Korea married women have been expected to stay at home. For a lot of women family and children are very important, so they prefer to focus on the family. I've become independent because I moved away from my family to go to college. I live away from home now and have a job. I think women should be able to work if they want to. My parents don't want me to work after I have a child, though.

**Kosuke, Japanese, 20**

In Japan, I think the expectations for both men and women are changing. In the past, only men were expected to **have a career** and support the family. Women were expected to raise the kids, cook, and clean. In my family though, my mom works and my father helps with the housework. As for me, I think I'd be miserable being a hardworking salaryman.

**Birte, German, 30**

These days, I think people expect men and women to be **equal**. Women are expected to be independent just like men. Things aren't always equal though. The government is mostly controlled by men. I live with my boyfriend, and I do more housework than he does. I complain about it to him sometimes.

1. What has traditionally been expected of married women in Korea?
2. How has Eun-suk become independent?
3. How does Kosuke feel about the idea of being a salaryman?
4. According to Birte, in Germany what is expected of women?
5. What does Birte complain to her boyfriend about?

## Speak Out

1. Pair work. Take turns asking your partner about gender roles.

A: Do you think it's good for (1) women to (2) stay at home?

B: (3) Yes, I do. (4) I think it's good for the children. But if fathers stay at home instead, I think that's good, too.

| 1 | 2 | 3 | 4 |
|---|---|---|---|
| men | stay at home | Yes, I do. | *Explain. Give extra information.* |
| women | be independent | No, I don't. | |
| | have a career | I'm not sure. | |

# FOCUS IN

What do you think about the differences between men and women? Circle your answers
in the questionnaire.

| | | | | |
|---|---|---|---|---|
| 1. | Do you think mothers are better parents than fathers? | Yes. | No. | I'm not sure. |
| 2. | Do you think men are better at business than women? | Yes. | No. | I'm not sure. |
| 3. | Do you think women are kinder than men? | Yes. | No. | I'm not sure. |
| 4. | Do you think men are more **logical** than women? | Yes. | No. | I'm not sure. |
| 5. | Do you think men should do more housework? | Yes. | No. | I'm not sure. |
| 6. | Do you think women and men should be totally equal? | Yes. | No. | I'm not sure. |

## Speak Out

1. Pair work. Take turns asking and answering the questions in Focus In.

   A: (1) Do you think mothers are better parents than fathers?

   B: (2) No, I don't. (3) It seems to me that (4) if you spend time with your children, you are
   a good parent. It's not important if you are the mother or the father.

| 1 | 2 | 3 | 4 |
|---|---|---|---|
| *Use a question from Focus In.* | No, I don't.<br>Yes, I do.<br>That's a hard question. | It seems to me that<br>In my family<br>I think | *Explain. Give extra information.* |

2. In your country, who **typically** does the following activities? Write male, female, or both.
   Then compare your answers with another classmate.

   _____ 1. handles the family's money
   _____ 2. **disciplines** the children
   _____ 3. cooks
   _____ 4. helps children with homework
   _____ 5. works full-time

# LISTEN IN

Listening 1

Listen to Judith and Paul talk about their careers. Are these statements *true* or *false*?
Listen and check (✓) the correct answers.

|  | True | False |
|---|---|---|
| 1. Judith wanted to become a flight attendant. | ____ | ____ |
| 2. There were many females in Judith's class. | ____ | ____ |
| 3. Paul is happy to be a stay-at-home dad. | ____ | ____ |
| 4. There are always other fathers at the playground. | ____ | ____ |

## Listening 2

Listen again and answer the questions.

1. How does Judith feel about being a pilot?

   _____

2. Why did Paul and his wife decide that one of them should stay home with their daughters?

   _____

## Speak Out

1. Read the list of professions. Which gender do you think is best suited to each one?
**Write *men*, *women*, or *both*.**

   _____ 1. nurse          _____ 3. lawyer            _____ 5. leader of a country
   _____ 2. musician       _____ 4. fashion designer  _____ 6. day care workers

2. **Pair work. Ask your partner which gender is suited to the professions in Speak Out 1.**

   A: Do you think (1) men make good (2) nurses?

   B: (3) Of course. (4) I think many men make good nurses because they are strong, but also gentle.

| 1 | 2 | 3 | 4 |
|---|---|---|---|
| men<br>women<br>both men and women | *Choose from the professions in Speak Out 1 above.* | Of course.<br>Absolutely not.<br>I'm not sure. | *Explain. Give extra information.* |

# FIND OUT MORE

 Read the passage, then answer the questions.

Margaret Mead was one of the first people to study the roles of men and women in different cultures. At 23, she went to Polynesia to study gender roles. She brought a woman's point of view to the study of culture and challenged traditional ideas about gender and sexuality.

Her studies of three different cultures in New Guinea—the Arapesh, the Mundugumor, and the Tchambuli—**convinced** her that gender roles are not determined by biology, but by our educational and **social environment**. For example, if we tell boys they shouldn't cry, we are training them to act in a certain way. Margaret Mead advised people to be more flexible about gender roles.

She also believed that the study of foreign cultures is a key to social progress

and understanding ourselves. She writes, "I have spent most of my life studying the lives of other peoples—faraway peoples—so that [we] might better understand ourselves."

1. How old was Margaret Mead when she first studied gender roles?
2. What ideas did she challenge?
3. What did she believe determines gender roles?
4. What did she advise people to do?
5. According to Margaret Mead, what is a key to social progress and understanding ourselves?

## Speak Out

**Pair work. Take turns talking about raising boys and girls.**

A: Do you think it's good to (1) tell sons that boys shouldn't cry?

B: (2) It depends. (3) Boys need to be strong, but girls need to be strong, too.

| 1 | 2 | 3 |
|---|---|---|
| tell sons that boys shouldn't cry | It depends. | *Explain. Give extra information.* |
| tell daughters that girls should be nice and not fight | Of course. | |
| encourage sons to play sports | I'm not sure. | |
| encourage daughters to wear dresses and look cute | Absolutely not. | |

 **Now do the Wrap Up Activity on page 71.**

# DIVERSITY

The different cultures that exist both within a country or region, and between cultures.

## FIND OUT

 Read the passage, then answer the questions.

**Rajiv, Indian, 35**

India is a very **diverse** country. We have many different languages, **dialects,** and ethnic groups in different regions of the country. If you want to better understand India, you should learn about our different **religions**. They are a big part of everyday life here. It's an important topic for us. We have Hindus, Muslims, Sikhs, Jains, Christians, and more. If you travel in India, don't be surprised if someone asks you about your religion.

**Theresa, Australian, 25**

In Australia, there are both **immigrants** and our native people, the Aborigines. When Europeans first arrived, the Aborigines had already been living here for 50,000 years. The immigrants often didn't appreciate Aboriginal culture, and much of it was destroyed. Fortunately, Australians value diversity more now. We encourage people from different countries to immigrate because these people have a wide range of knowledge and skills that benefit our country.

**Min-Jin, Korean, 32**

The different regions of Korea have their own special qualities that people there are proud of. People from the western part are said to be good at traditional arts. People from the eastern part have the **reputation** of being very social and outgoing. Also, different areas have different accents, so people can often tell where you come from as soon as you start talking to them.

1. What might people ask you about if you travel in India?
2. What happened to Aboriginal culture?
3. Why do Australians encourage people from different countries to immigrate?
4. What is the reputation of people from the western part of Korea?
5. What can people often tell from different accents?

## Speak Out

Pair work. Take turns asking each other about diversity in your country.

A: How much do you know about the different (1)  ethnic groups here?

B: (2) Very little. (3) I know the Ainu live in Hokkaido, but I don't know much about their culture.

| 1 | | 2 | 3 |
|---|---|---|---|
| ethnic groups | religions | Very little. | *Explain. Give extra information.* |
| languages | special regions | A little. | |
| dialects | | A lot. | |

# FOCUS IN

Think about the diversity in your country. Do you have a strong interest in it? Circle your answers in the questionnaire and find out.

|  | Yes. | Somewhat. | Not really. |
|---|---|---|---|
| 1. Do you enjoy listening to traditional music? | 1 | 2 | 3 |
| 2. Do you have an interest in learning about different religions? | 1 | 2 | 3 |
| 3. Do you enjoy trying special food from different regions? | 1 | 2 | 3 |
| 4. Do you enjoy traditional festivals and **celebrations**? | 1 | 2 | 3 |
| 5. Do you enjoy traveling to different parts of the country? | 1 | 2 | 3 |
| 6. Do you know about the culture of different ethnic groups? | 1 | 2 | 3 |

**Add your score to find out how much interest in diversity you have.**

**6 – 10    You have a lot of interest in diversity.**

**11 – 14   You have some interest in diversity.**

**15 – 18   You have little interest in diversity.**

## Speak Out

Pair work. Take turns talking about each other's answers in Focus In.

A: What was your result?

B: According to my score, I have (1) a lot of interest in diversity.

A: So, (2) do you enjoy traditional festivals and celebrations?

B: (3) Yes, a lot. (4) I love going to local festivals in my hometown. It makes me proud of its history and culture.

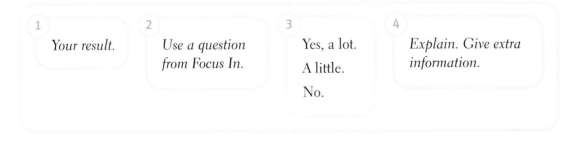

| 1 | 2 | 3 | 4 |
|---|---|---|---|
| Your result. | Use a question from Focus In. | Yes, a lot. A little. No. | Explain. Give extra information. |

# LISTEN IN

## Listening 1

Stereotypes are ideas we have about people who are different from us. Listen to Yuko and David give their opinions about stereotypes. Which ideas do they mention? Write *Y* for Yuko and *D* for David.

**Yuko, Japanese, 29**    **David, American, 27**

_____ 1. It's normal for people to have stereotypes of others.
_____ 2. Stereotypes are caused by the media and movies.
_____ 3. Stereotyping makes it harder for people to get to know you.
_____ 4. Some stereotypes are **positive** and others are **negative**.
_____ 5. People thought that all Americans were rich.

## Listening 2

Listen again and complete the sentences.

1. Why does Yuko think it's important to have an open mind toward other cultures?

   _____

2. How can people get over stereotypes?

   _____

## Speak Out

1. Do these stereotypes exist about young people in your country? Write Y for yes or N for no. Add your own idea.

   Young people ...
   _____ 1. love loud music.
   _____ 2. are not respectful of their parents and other older people.
   _____ 3. are wild (love to go to parties, dances, etc.).
   _____ 4. are very interested in fashion.
   _____ 5. are good at using computers.
   _____ 6. only want to have fun.
   _____ 7. Your idea: _____

2. Pair work. Take turns asking these questions about stereotypes.

   A: What do you think of the stereotype "Young people (1) love loud music"?

   B: Well, I think this is (2) somewhat true. (3) It depends on the person. Some people may think this because they see young people listening to loud rock music.

   | 1 | 2 | 3 |
   |---|---|---|
   | *Choose from the statements in Speak Out 1.* | somewhat true<br><br>very true<br><br>not at all true | *Explain. Give extra information.* |

# FIND OUT MORE

Read the passage, then answer the questions.

**Hal Glatzer**, a journalist and novelist who worked in Hawaii for 11 years, says that it is an **inspiring** example of harmony in a **multicultural** environment. There are many races in Hawaii but little **racism**. What can the rest of us learn from this example?

"Know who you are. It is not considered rude in Hawaii to ask about someone's race. At a party, I heard a Haole (white person) ask an Asian who had just said his name, 'Are you a Chinese 'L-i' or a Korean 'L-e-e'?' In Hawaii, you are expected to be proud of your ancestry, and to share the pride of others in theirs.

"Laugh at your stereotype. Stereotypes are a starting point for the getting-to-know-you process. In Hawaii, the stereotypes are: Haoles are rich, Chinese are **stingy**, Japanese are **bureaucratic**, Hawaiians are lazy, and Samoans are **fierce**. Yet everyone knows people who don't fit these descriptions at all.

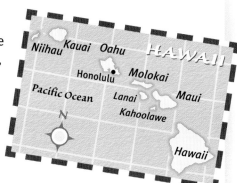

"Share one another's culture. Some children in Hawaii study ballet, but practically every kid learns hula. Most people play sports, but quite a few pursue the Asian **martial arts** as well. There are as many Haoles and other races as there are Japanese in a summertime Bon dance.

"Share your children. Every child in Hawaii has friends from other ethnic groups. The shared experience of being a 'local' boy or girl is not based on your ethnicity but on where you go to school."

1. Why is Hawaii an inspiring example of harmony in a multicultural environment?
2. What are you expected to be proud of in Hawaii?
3. What are stereotypes a starting point for?
4. Who learns hula in Hawaii?
5. What is being a "local" boy or girl based on?

## Speak Out

Pair work. Talk about Hal Glatzer's four pieces of advice. Do they help people better understand diversity? Give your opinion about each one.

*Example:*

I think that "Know who you are" is good advice. Learning about our history, our traditions, and our art gives us something to be proud of. If we are proud of our culture, we can share it with other people.

 Now do the Wrap Up Activity on page 72.

# SOCIAL CHANGE

Change that makes society and the world a better place.

## FIND OUT

 Read the passage, then answer the questions.

**Michel, French, 55**

   I think life is better now, in modern times, than in the past. We're richer than before, have better technology, and society has become more equal. For example, in the past women were expected to stay at home, and if you were born poor, you stayed poor. We've had to struggle for a long time to change things like that and make the world a better place for everyone. We should get rid of unfair attitudes from the past like **prejudice**. We still have a lot of problems, like **poverty**, but we're making progress and I think the future for people in the world is bright.

**Jai Min, Korean, 56**

   These days, open the newspaper and you'll see problems like crime, a high **divorce** rate, and drug use. I think a lot of this is caused by our modern lifestyle. Even though modern technology like computers and cell phones make life convenient, I think we've lost many good traditional values. For example, students would rather play video games than study, nobody knows their neighbors, and young people are losing respect for their elders. I think that too much money and convenience make people selfish and we must **hold on to** the good things from the past.

1. In what ways does Michel feel life is better now than in the past?
2. According to Michel, in what ways was life worse in the past?
3. What does Michel think about the future?
4. According to Jai Min, what causes the problems in society today?
5. What examples does Jai Min give of our loss of traditions and values?

## Speak Out

**Pair work. Take turns talking about Michel and Jai Min's opinions.**

A: Do you think (1) life is better in modern times?

B: (2) Yes, I guess so. (3) Cell phones and e-mail let us communicate with people everywhere conveniently.

| 1 | 2 | 3 |
|---|---|---|
| life is better in modern times | Yes, I guess so. | *Explain. Give extra information.* |
| there's less prejudice today | Well, not really. | |
| we've lost many traditional values | That could be. | |

# FOCUS IN

What social problems is your society facing? Check (✓) the answers in the questionnaire.

| How serious are these social problems? | Very serious. | Somewhat serious. | Not so serious. |
|---|---|---|---|
| 1. crime and violence | ____ | ____ | ____ |
| 2. **bullying** and youth problems | ____ | ____ | ____ |
| 3. **discrimination** and prejudice | ____ | ____ | ____ |
| 4. the loss of tradition | ____ | ____ | ____ |
| 5. divorce and family problems | ____ | ____ | ____ |
| 6. lack of equality for women | ____ | ____ | ____ |

## Speak Out

1. Pair work. Take turns discussing your answers in Focus In.

   A: Do you think our society has a problem with (1) crime and violence?

   B: (2) Absolutely. (3) I think the problem is very serious. These days we often see stories about crime in the newspaper.

| 1 | 2 | 3 |
|---|---|---|
| *Use a phrase from Focus In.* | Absolutely. <br> I think so. <br> I'm not sure. <br> Not really. | *Explain. Give extra information.* |

2. Presentation. Write your answers to these questions: What traditional values do you think are important to keep? What social problems can they help us solve? Share your ideas with your classmates.

   *Example:*

   The problem of students not going to school would improve if young people had more respect for education.

   _____

   _____

# LISTEN IN

🔘 Listening 1

Listen to three people talk about their experiences with discrimination. Check (✓) the subjects they mention.

**Charles, British, 26**

**Miki, Japanese, 21**

**Jing, Chinese, 27**

| | | |
|---|---|---|
| ____ body type | ____ gender | |
| ____ race | ____ religion | |
| ____ country | ____ age | |

🔘 Listening 2

Listen again and complete the sentences.

1. What does Charles think we have to teach children?

    _____

2. What ideas does Miki's father have about foreign countries?

    _____

3. What does Jing feel is unfair?

    _____

## Speak Out

1. Pair work. Take turns talking about discrimination in your country.

    A: Do you think that discrimination based on (1) body type is a problem?

    B: (2) Yes, it's somewhat of a problem. (3) In school, I saw kids bullied because they were fat.

| 1 | 2 | 3 |
|---|---|---|
| *Choose from the items in Listening 1.* | Yes, it's a big problem. <br> Yes, it's somewhat of a problem. <br> No, it's not much of a problem. | *Explain. Give extra information.* |

2. Pair work. What would you do in the situations below? Write your answers, then share them with another pair.

    1. You see students bullying a student who looks different. _____

    2. You want to study abroad, but your parents say no because they feel that foreign countries are unsafe.

    _____

# FIND OUT MORE

 Read the passage, then answer the questions.

Nelson Mandela was a **political activist** and lawyer in South Africa. He spent 24 years in prison because of his fight for equal rights for all races. When he was released from prison, he was elected the president of South Africa and received the Nobel Peace Prize. In this passage he tells of the moment he was arrested.

"Just after dawn on the morning of December 5, 1956, I was woken by a loud knocking on my door. No neighbor or friend ever knocks in such a way, and I knew immediately that it was the security police.

"They immediately began to look through the entire house for papers or documents. By this time, the children were awake and I told them to be calm. They looked to me for **reassurance**. After 45 minutes, I was told, 'Mandela, we have a **warrant** for your arrest. Come with me.'

"I walked with them to the car. It is not pleasant to be arrested in front of one's children, even though one knows that what one is doing is right. But children do not comprehend the **complexity** of the situation; they simply see their father being taken away by the white **authorities** without an explanation."

1. Who was Nelson Mandela?
2. Why did Mandela spend 24 years in prison?
3. What happened after he got out of prison?
4. How did he know that the security police were at the door?
5. What were the police looking for?

## Speak Out

Pair work. Answer the questions below about your country. Use the ideas you learned in this unit. Then share your answers with another pair.

1. What are the two biggest social problems in your country?
2. How do you think they can be solved?
3. Why are they important to you?

 **Now do the Wrap Up Activity on page 72.**

# GLOBAL COMMUNITY

A global community is formed when people from various cultures have good relationships with each other.

## FIND OUT

Read the passage, then answer the questions.

**Peter, German, 30**

When someone asks me where I come from, I say "everywhere." My parents are German, but I was born in Nepal because my father was a **diplomat**. I grew up in India, Germany, the United States, and Argentina. I speak Hindi, German, English, French, and Spanish. People like me are sometimes called "third culture kids" because our identity doesn't come from one or two places, but from everywhere we've lived. People everywhere are different. To become a **global citizen** you need to live abroad and learn foreign languages so that you can see the world from different points of view.

**Sarie, South African, 40**

I grew up in a very small town in South Africa but I always wanted to see the world. I became a doctor and started working in public health, in particular the **prevention** of childhood diseases. Through my research and medical volunteer work I have visited more than 30 countries. I love meeting new people wherever I go. The most important thing for being a global citizen is simply to have an open mind. It lets you see that in spite of any cultural differences, people everywhere have the same feelings and needs. If you smile, people will smile back at you.

1. Why did Peter grow up in so many different places?
2. Why are people like Peter called "third culture kids"?
3. What does Peter think you need to become a global citizen?
4. What does Sarie think is most important for being a global citizen?
5. Why does Sarie feel it's important to have an open mind?

## Speak Out

Pair work. Take turns discussing Peter and Sarie's opinions.

A: (1) Peter says that (2) people everywhere are different. What do you think?

B: I think (3) that's true. (4) Every country has its own values and lifestyles.

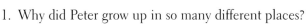

| 1 | 2 | 3 | 4 |
|---|---|---|---|
| Peter | people everywhere are different | that's true | *Explain. Give extra information.* |
| Sarie | people everywhere have the same feelings and needs | it depends | |
| | to be a global citizen you simply need to have an open mind | *Your idea:* _____ | |

# FOCUS IN

What kind of global citizen are you? Circle your answers in the questionnaire to find out.

|  | No. | Maybe. | Yes. |
|---|---|---|---|
| Would you like to ... | | | |
| 1. volunteer for an international organization? | 1 | 2 | 3 |
| 2. live in another country for at least a year? | 1 | 2 | 3 |
| 3. start to learn a new foreign language? | 1 | 2 | 3 |
| 4. marry someone from a different country? | 1 | 2 | 3 |
| 5. raise your family abroad? | 1 | 2 | 3 |
| 6. work for a foreign company? | 1 | 2 | 3 |

**Add your score to find out what kind of global citizen you are.**
**14 – 18   You are an adventurous global citizen.**
**10 – 13   You are a curious global citizen.**
**6 – 9      You are a careful global citizen.**

## Speak Out

1. Pair work. Take turns talking about each other's results.

> A: What's your result?
>
> B: According to the questionnaire, I'm a (1) curious global citizen.
>
> A: So, would you like to (2) volunteer for an international organization?
>
> B: That sounds (3) **fascinating**. (4) I could meet many people, and help others, too.

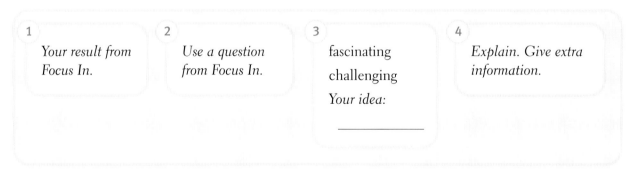

| 1 | 2 | 3 | 4 |
|---|---|---|---|
| *Your result from Focus In.* | *Use a question from Focus In.* | fascinating<br>challenging<br>*Your idea:*<br>_____ | *Explain. Give extra information.* |

2. Choose the two items from Focus In that you would most like to try. Why? Write your answers, then share them with classmates.

_____

_____

# LISTEN IN

Listening 1

Pedro Rivera is an international businessman. Listen to him talk about making conversation with people from other countries. Write Y for the topics he says are OK, and N for the topics he says to be careful about.

| ____ politics | ____ fashion | ____ salary | ____ music | ____ food |
| ____ computers | ____ movies | ____ technology | ____ religion | ____ age |

Listening 2

What advice does the speaker give? Listen again and write your answer.

1. What is the key to international business? _____

2. What do we share with people in other countries? _____

## Speak Out

1. Pair work. Take turns talking about which topics from Listening 1 are common in your country.

A: Do you think (1) movies is a common topic?

B: (2) Yes, I do. (3) I often hear people talking about movies they have seen.

| 1 | 2 | 3 |
|---|---|---|
| A *topic from Listening 1.* | Yes, I do. No, I don't. | *Explain. Give extra information.* |

2. Pair work. Take turns talking about which of the topics in Listening 1 you enjoy talking about.

A: Do you enjoy talking about (1) movies?

B: (2) Yes, I do. (3) I see a lot of movies, so I have a lot to talk about.

| 1 | 2 | 3 |
|---|---|---|
| A *topic from Listening 1.* | Yes, I do. No, I don't. | *Explain. Give extra information.* |

# FIND OUT MORE

Read the passage, then answer the questions.

**Mahatma Gandhi** was a religious and political leader during India's fight for independence from Britain. It was a difficult struggle because not only did India have to fight against Britain, it also faced problems of poverty, discrimination, and ethnic conflict. In the end, his leadership helped bring millions of people together to create a diverse and democratic India in 1947.

Gandhi was a Hindu and had a strong sense of right and wrong, but he showed great flexibility toward other beliefs and cultures. He even admired many things about British culture. At the same time, he had confidence in his own vision. Gandhi's personal philosophy about global community can be found in this **quote**: "I want the cultures of all lands to be blown about my house as freely as possible. But I refuse to be blown off my feet by any."

In this quote, Gandhi says that he wants to live in a house with open windows that allow the wind of other cultures and new ideas to blow in. At the same time, he refuses to be "blown off his feet" by the winds of difference. He stands firmly. Gandhi's ideas teach us two lessons: learn from diversity and be proud of who you are. It's a good philosophy for building a global community.

1. Who was Mahatma Gandhi?
2. What kind of problems did India face?
3. What did Gandhi's leadership help accomplish?
4. How did Gandhi feel about other beliefs and cultures?
5. What are the two lessons that Gandhi's philosophy teaches us?

## Speak Out

1. What are the qualities that great leaders need? Check (✓) your answers and add your own idea.

| | | |
|---|---|---|
| ____ an outgoing personality | ____ **confidence** in yourself | Your idea: |
| ____ a sense of right and wrong | ____ great intelligence | _____ |

2. Pair work. Take turns talking about the qualities of great leaders.

A: I think (1) <u>an outgoing personality</u> is important for a leader. What do you think?

B: (2) <u>I agree.</u> (3) <u>If you are shy, people won't follow you.</u>

| 1 | 2 | 3 |
|---|---|---|
| *Use a phrase from Speak Out 1.* | I agree. I disagree. I'm not sure. | *Explain. Give extra information.* |

**Now do the Wrap Up Activity on page 73.**

# TAPESCRIPT

## Unit 1

### FIND OUT

See reading passage on page 2.

### LISTEN IN

See page 4.

**Chiho:** My father is Italian and my mother is Japanese. When I was a child, I spent about half my time in Japan and half in Italy. I had Italian friends and relatives and Japanese friends and relatives. When I change languages, I guess I change how I act. When I speak Italian, I am more expressive and move my hands a lot. My communication style is different.

Sometimes I meet people for the first time in Italy and they have a certain image of how I should be—you know, like a shy and serious Japanese girl. And in Japan, sometimes people have an image of Italians as outgoing and fun loving. So they expect me to be that way.

It's kind of funny, but I think there are two sides to my identity—an Italian side and a Japanese side. But of course there's only *one* Chiho!

### FIND OUT MORE

See reading passage on page 5.

# Unit 2

## FIND OUT

See reading passage on page 6.

## LISTEN IN

See page 8.

**Patricia:** When I was a child, one thing I was not allowed to do was lie. I was always told that lying is worse than stealing. My mother used to say that by telling the truth, we show respect to ourselves and respect to other people. Once, my mother caught me telling a lie. She told me that when you lie, you are being dishonest with the person you are lying to and you are being dishonest with yourself. And that is the worst thing of all. I learned the values of honesty and respect from my mother.

**Ravi:** From the time I was a child, I was told to act like a gentleman. There was a rule in our house that my brother and I should not fight over small things, like sharing toys. It wasn't until I was older that I understood the value of thinking about the important things—not little things that don't matter, like fighting over toys. My family taught me to value manners and cooperation—things I use in my life every day now.

**Nicole:** I grew up on a horse farm in New Zealand. When I was ten years old, I wanted my own pony. I promised my parents that I would take care of it and be responsible for it. Finally, they gave me one. It was a lot of work, and after a few weeks I told my parents that they could have the pony back. They said that I had asked for the pony and I had to take care of it. Later I realized that my parents taught me the value of keeping promises and being responsible.

## FIND OUT MORE

See reading passage on page 9.

# Unit 3

## FIND OUT

See reading passage on page 10.

## LISTEN IN

See page 12.

**Vincent:** If you ever visit Paris, you may find that some things are less convenient than in your country. For example, there are only a few vending machines and big rental video stores in Paris. Also, most businesses are closed in the evenings, so you have to shop during the day. In the evenings, French people often go out with their friends or family. So if you live in Paris, you should go out to a sidewalk cafe or restaurant in the evenings instead of watching videos at home.

Oh, you need to know greetings. Don't be surprised if someone kisses you on both cheeks. And handshakes—we often shake hands even with friends that we see every day. Also, you should greet shopkeepers and store clerks. If not, you will seem rude. Just say *bonjour*! They will be friendlier to you.

Finally, even if you don't speak French well, why don't you try learning at least a little? It's good to bring a phrase book and learn a few words before you come. People will talk to you more, and you will make friends much faster. I think making friends is the most important thing for getting along in a new country.

## FIND OUT MORE

See reading passage on page 13.

# Unit 4

## FIND OUT

See reading passage on page 14.

## LISTEN IN

See page 16.

**Yoshi:** Robert, what's the matter? You look angry.

**Robert:** I am angry. I'm *really* angry.

**Yoshi:** Why? What's wrong?

**Robert:** I'll tell you, but keep it under your hat, OK?

**Yoshi:** Excuse me? I don't wear a hat.

**Robert:** Oh, sorry. I mean, don't tell anyone about this. Do you know Alan? Yesterday I saw him with my girlfriend, Angela, in front of the movie theater. You know I'm crazy about her.

**Yoshi:** What? You're crazy?

**Robert:** No. I mean I really love her. And yesterday, she was with my best friend.

**Yoshi:** Did they see you?

**Robert:** No. So I asked him later what he was doing. He said he just saw Angela on the street and they were talking. It sounded fishy to me, though.

**Yoshi:** What? A fish? Where?

**Robert:** There's no fish! I mean, I didn't think he was telling me the truth.

**Yoshi:** Oh, so what did you do?

**Robert:** I blew my top—I mean I started yelling at him.

**Yoshi:** You did? What did he do?

**Robert:** He yelled back. He told me that I was wrong.

**Yoshi:** Maybe you should trust Alan more. He is your friend.

**Robert:** Maybe you're right …

## FIND OUT MORE

See reading passage on page 17.

# Unit 5

## FIND OUT

See reading passage on page 18.

## LISTEN IN

See page 20.

**Jerzy:** When people go to someone's house for dinner in Poland, they typically bring flowers. It is important to bring an **odd number** of flowers because an even number is considered bad luck. You should also greet each person individually. Waving at a group of people to say hello or good-bye is considered rude.

**Leena:** In India, we greet Hindus by using *namaste*. We hold our hands together in front of our chests. It's a greeting, but we also use it to say good-bye. We don't really touch each other as much as Americans do. For example, friends don't hug each other a lot when they meet.

**Stephanie:** In Greece, when you go to someone's house for dinner, you don't have to arrive exactly on time. Social events like parties often begin at least an hour after the set time and have no fixed ending time. Everyone talks at the same time and people even interrupt one another. Don't worry about jumping into the conversation—everyone does!

## FIND OUT MORE

See reading passage on page 21.

# Unit 6

## FIND OUT

See reading passage on page 22.

## LISTEN IN

See page 24.

**Naoko:** In Japan, people in the same company sometimes go out together after work. I go out with my co-workers at least once a week. It's good because we get to know each other better. That makes working together a lot easier. Friends from our school days are also important. I get together every year with my high-school friends. It's great because we have a lot to talk about and these get-togethers are always exciting.

**Ahmed:** Malaysia is a very interesting country. We have three ethnic groups: Malay, Chinese, and Indian. Each one has its own special traditions and culture. There are a lot of cultural differences in Malaysia, but one thing that is important to all of us is family. Family relationships are valuable because you can always **count on** your family. And, of course, your family knows you better than anyone else does!

## FIND OUT MORE

See reading passage on page 25.

# Unit 7

## FIND OUT

See reading passage on page 26.

## LISTEN IN

See page 28.

**Mohamed:** When I was in high school, I had a science teacher who I respected deeply because he was hardworking, passionate, and really cared about his students. He changed my life. Because of him, I became a scientist. In Egypt teachers receive a lot of respect, and when a teacher enters the room, students stop talking and stand up. Also, when students meet a teacher on the street, they are expected to bow politely. My science teacher certainly **deserved** such respect.

**Cameron:** I respect my father a lot. He is a police officer here in London. He is very serious about his work, but he is also an easygoing person and likes to tell jokes. People call him "Chuck" instead of "Sergeant Maxwell." Of course, I don't call him by his first name; I call him "dad." And I always listen to what he says. Oh, and one other thing—I always look him in the eye when he's telling me something important.

## FIND OUT MORE

See reading passage on page 29.

# Unit 8

## FIND OUT

See reading passage on page 30.

## LISTEN IN

See page 32.

**John:** When I started working at my company, a long-time employee, Keiko, thought I was making mistakes in my work. It's true that I had problems learning my new job, but I didn't think it was so serious. Instead of telling me **to my face**, openly, that she was concerned, Keiko talked to my boss. She might have been embarrassed to say something to me directly, but I didn't like it. I prefer communication that's direct and honest, especially if there's a problem.

**Keiko:** When John started working here, he tried hard, but it took him a long time to learn how to do his job. In the beginning, I could see that he was making a lot of mistakes. He's older than I am, and I didn't want to hurt his feelings by saying something. I explained the situation to our boss and didn't mention the problem to John directly. John didn't like that because he felt that I was talking **behind his back**. I wish he understood that I was trying to protect his feelings.

## FIND OUT MORE

See reading passage on page 33.

# Unit 9

## FIND OUT

See reading passage on page 34.

## LISTEN IN

See page 36.

**Judith:** I'm a pilot. I fly commercial jets from the United States to Asia, Europe ... everywhere! I always wanted to fly, but growing up I never saw any female pilots. Even today there are many more male pilots than female pilots. When I entered the classroom on the first day of pilot school, I was surprised to see that I was the only woman in the room. However, I finished pilot school and **achieved** my childhood dream. I love it and I feel proud that I'm in this profession. This is a great job, so I hope more women will join me.

**Paul:** I'm a stay-at-home dad. When our daughters were born, we decided that one of us should stay at home with them because we didn't want to take them to a **day-care center** or leave them with a baby-sitter. My wife is a lawyer and makes a great salary and loves her career. I was working then, too, but I really love kids and was happy to **quit** my job. So it was clear to us that I should stay home. It's a lot of work, but I don't **regret** it. Being a good parent is really hard. It's a big responsibility, but also very rewarding. When I take my kids to the playground, I feel strange because I'm the only father there, but I get to share a lot of wonderful times with my daughters. If you're working ten hours a day, there are many special moments that you miss.

## FIND OUT MORE

See reading passage on page 37.

# Unit 10

## FIND OUT

See reading passage on page 38.

## LISTEN IN

See page 40.

**Yuko:** Of course everyone has some simple images and ideas about people from countries they've never visited. For example, in Japan a lot of people think Italians are passionate and that the French are romantic and good cooks. Sometimes these stereotypes are positive, and sometimes they're negative. I guess it's normal for people to have stereotypes of other cultures if they've never been there. Of course, not everyone from one culture is the same. People and cultures are not that simple. That's why keeping an open mind toward other cultures is important.

**David:** I'm from the United States. When I traveled around the world last summer, I found people who thought that all Americans were rich. It was strange to hear this because in America I'm certainly not rich. I think that a lot of stereotypes are caused by the media and movies. If you only see other cultures on TV or in movies, you don't get a very balanced view of them. A lot of times stereotypes are negative. It's hard for people to get to know me if they start with a negative image of Americans. To **get over** stereotypes, I think you have to travel and really experience other countries.

## FIND OUT MORE

See reading passage on page 41.

# Unit 11

## FIND OUT

See reading passage on page 42.

## LISTEN IN

See page 44.

**Charles:** In elementary school, there was a girl who was very big. Many kids were really cruel to her. They teased her and called her "fat." I feel ashamed to admit that I teased her sometimes, too. Kids can be cruel when one child is different from the rest. We have to teach children that everyone has feelings, so there's no excuse for bullying.

**Miki:** Recently, my parents made me feel really angry. When I told them I wanted to go study English in a foreign country, they immediately said, "No, foreign countries are not safe for young women." They never even asked me which country! My father has this idea that foreigners are dangerous, and that other countries are full of drugs and crime. But those ideas are just stereotypes. He's never even been out of the country!

**Jing:** When I tried to get a job after graduating from college, being a woman made it very difficult. My male friends got jobs quickly, but it took me a long, long time. I felt so frustrated. My male friends and I went to the same university, took the same courses, and had equal ability. So why should they have an advantage? It's also unfair that companies sometimes assume that all women will quit their jobs when they have children. That's not true. Companies should make it easier for women to work when they have families.

## FIND OUT MORE

See reading passage on page 45.

# Unit 12

## FIND OUT

See reading passage on page 46.

## LISTEN IN

See page 48.

**Pedro Rivera:** I work for an international software company and I deal with customers from over 40 different countries. Because good relationships are the key to international business, I've had to learn how to get along with people from all over the world. I've learned to look for points in common and use them to make conversation. When you have a common interest with people, you naturally have good feelings about them.

The Internet and international media bring news and information everywhere, so there are a lot of common topics, like music, food, movies, or fashion. Of course, I work in a high-tech industry so I talk a lot about technology and computers. You should be careful, though. In some places you shouldn't bring up topics like politics, religion, age, and salary, unless you know the people very well.

When I first traveled in foreign countries, everything seemed **exotic**, like the buildings, clothes, or food … but I realized that the people in those buildings, wearing those clothes, eating that food, well, they share a lot with me. For example, people everywhere have families and friends. We all need to work, and we all like to have fun. If we find the things we have in common, we can all get along.

## FIND OUT MORE

See reading passage on page 49.

# GLOSSARY

## Unit 1

**summer-abroad program** (n.): an arrangement in which students study in a foreign country during summer vacation

**assignment** (n.): a task or piece of work that someone is given to do, usually as part of their job or studies

**vague** (adj.): not clear in a person's mind; not having or giving enough information or details about something

**grade** (n.): a mark given on an exam or for a piece of schoolwork

**pleasing**: making someone happy

**outgoing** (adj.): enjoying meeting other people and their company, and being friendly toward them

**traditional** (adj.): beliefs, customs, or ways of life that have not changed for a long time

**intercultural communication** (n.): communication that takes place between people who come from different cultures

**conflict** (n.): a situation in which people, groups, or countries are involved in a serious disagreement or argument

## Unit 2

**values** (n.): beliefs about what is right and wrong and what is important in life

**insisted** (v.): demanded that something happens or that someone agrees to do something

**give in to**: to agree to do something that you do not want to do

**stand up for**: to support or defend someone/something

**responsibility** (n.): a duty to deal with or take care of someone/something; having to be held accountable for someone/something

**selfish** (adj.): caring only about yourself rather than about other people

**stable** (adj.): firmly fixed; not likely to move, change, or fail

**cooperation** (n.): doing something together or working together toward a shared aim

**messy** (adj.): dirty and/or untidy

**guaranteed** (adj.): something promised or certain to occur

# Unit 3

**unfamiliar** (adj.): someone/something you do not know or recognize

**keep up with**: to maintain a level of understanding in a conversation

**speak up**: to say what you think clearly and freely, especially in order to support or defend someone/something

**depressed** (adj.): very sad and without hope

**get to know**: to learn about or become acquainted with someone/something

**stood out**: had certain characteristics that caused one to be noticeably different

**flexible** (adj.): able to change to suit new conditions or situations

**adapt** (v.): to change your behavior in order to deal more successfully with a new situation

**Peace Corps** (n.): an organization that sends people to work as volunteers in countries in need

**intercultural training** (n.): teaching skills for effective communication with people from other cultures

# Unit 4

**none of your business**: something that does not concern you

**squeaky** (adj.): something that makes a short, high sound

**ventured** (v.): to have gone somewhere or done something even though you knew that it might be dangerous or unpleasant

**reflect on**: to think carefully and deeply about something

**remorse** (n.): the feeling of being extremely sorry for something wrong or bad that you have done

**genuine** (adj.): sincere and honest; able to be trusted

# Unit 5

**hugged** (v.): to have put your arms around someone and held them tightly, especially to show that you like or love them

**embarrassed** (adj.): felt shy, awkward, or ashamed, especially in a social situation

**odd number** (n.): a number that cannot be divided exactly by the number two (1, 3, 5, and 7 are odd numbers); the opposite of an even number

**odd** (adj.): strange or unusual

**cool** (adj.): what people say to show that they approve of something or agree to a suggestion

# Unit 6

**individualism** (n.): the belief that individual people in society should have the right to make their own decisions, etc.

**collectivist** (n.): someone who emphasizes the importance of personal relationships within a group, rather than individualism

**one-on-one** (adj.): between two people only

**count on**: to depend on or to trust someone to do something

**ethnic** (adj.): connected with or belonging to a nation, race, or tribe that shares a cultural tradition

**credit** (n.): praise or approval given to one who is responsible for something good that has happened

**uncooperative** (adj.): not willing to be helpful to other people or do what they ask

# Unit 7

**courtesy** (n.): polite behavior that shows respect for other people

**polite language** (n.): special words or sentence patterns used to show good manners, respect, or humility

**formal** (adj.): very correct and suitable for official or important occasions

**casually** (adv.): not showing much care or thought; not wanting to show that something is important to you

**deserved** (v.): having the right to something because of the way you behave or who you are

**bow** (v.): to move your head or the top half of your body forward and downward as a sign of respect or as a greeting

**etiquette** (n.): the formal rules of correct or polite behavior in society or among members of a particular profession

**suppress** (v.): to prevent yourself from having or expressing a feeling or an emotion

# Unit 8

**expressive** (adj.): showing or able to show your thoughts and feelings

**reserved** (adj.): slow or unwilling to show feelings or express opinions

**upset** (adj.): unhappy, anxious, or annoyed

**subtle** (adj.): not very noticeable or obvious

**emotional** (adj.): showing strong emotions, sometimes in a way that other people think is unnecessary

**to my face**: directly, in person

**behind his back**: without someone's knowledge

**colleague** (n.): people that you work with, especially in a profession or a business

**neutral** (adj.): not expressing feelings openly

**plainly** (adv.): in a simple way

# Unit 9

**gender** (n.): all the things related to being male or female

**have a career**: to be a professional; to work rather than stay at home

**equal** (adj.): having the same rights or being treated the same way as other people, without differences such as race, religion, or sex being considered

**logical** (adj.): following or able to follow the rules of logic in which ideas or facts are based on other true ideas or facts

**typically** (adv.): in a way that shows the usual qualities or features of a particular type of person, thing, or group

**disciplines** (v.): trains people to obey rules and orders and punishes them if they do not

**achieved** (v.): succeeded in reaching a particular goal, status, or standard, especially by making an effort for a long time

**day-care center** (n.): a place which offers child care, usually as a service offered by a business, a government, or an organization

**quit** (v.): to leave your job, school, etc.

**regret** (v.): to feel sorry about something you have done or about something that you have not been able to do

**convinced** (v.): made someone/yourself believe that something is true

**social environment** (n.): one's surroundings, the people or society that one lives in or grows up in

# Unit 10

**diverse** (adj.): composed of people of various religions, ethnic groups, etc.

**dialects** (n.): forms of the same language that may contain variations in grammar, words, and pronunciation

**religions** (n.): different beliefs in the existence of a god or gods, and the activities that are connected with the worship of them

**immigrants** (n.): people who have come to live permanently in a country that is not their own

**reputation** (n.): the opinion that people have about what someone/something is like, based on what has happened in the past

**celebrations** (n.): special events that people organize in order to celebrate something

**get over**: to overcome or get past a misunderstanding or mistaken impression

**positive** (adj.): having a good meaning or effect

**negative** (adj.): having a bad meaning or effect

**inspiring** (adj.): exciting and encouraging one to do or feel something

**multicultural** (adj.): including people of several different races, religions, languages, and traditions

**racism** (n.): the unfair treatment of people who belong to a different race; violent behavior toward them

**stingy** (adj.): not given or giving willingly; not generous, especially with money

**bureaucratic** (adj.): connected with a bureaucracy or bureaucrats and involving complicated official rules which may seem unnecessary

**fierce** (adj.): showing strong feelings or a lot of activity, often in a way that is violent

**martial arts** (n.): any of the self-defense arts that are practiced as sports, including judo and karate

# Unit 11

prejudice (n.): an unreasonable dislike of or preference for a person, group, custom, etc., especially when it is based on their race, religion, sex, etc.

poverty (n.): the state of being poor

divorce (n.): the legal ending of a marriage

hold on to: to keep something; to not give or sell something to someone else

bullying (v.): frightening or hurting a weaker person; using your strength or power to make someone do something

discrimination (n.): the practice of treating someone or a particular group in society less fairly than others

political activist (n.): a person who works to achieve political change

reassurance (n.): the fact of giving advice or help that takes away a person's fears or doubts

warrant (n.): a legal document that gives police some special power, such as to arrest someone or search their house

complexity (n.): the features of a problem or situation that are difficult to understand

authorities (n.): police officers or other government officials who hold the power in a certain situation

# Unit 12

diplomat (n.): a person whose job it is to represent his or her country in a foreign country, for example, in an embassy

global citizen (n.): someone who actively tries to have good relationships with people from other countries and cultures

prevention (n.): the act of stopping something from happening

fascinating (adj.): very attractive or interesting

exotic (adj.): seeming exciting and unusual because it is connected with foreign countries

quote (n.): the exact words that another person has said or written

confidence (n.): a belief in your own ability to do things and be successful

# WRAP UP ACTIVITIES

 ## Unit 1: Wrap Up

Prepare a short presentation on culture and identity. Share your ideas with other students. Use these questions to help you:

What is important to you?

What experiences have affected you?

What is your experience with cultural difference?

Do you have a strong cultural identity?

What similarities or differences do you have with your peers?

What career do you want to pursue, and why?

Would you ever live in another country? Why or why not?

What are some of your hidden and visible cultural differences?

 ## Unit 2: Wrap Up

Prepare a short presentation on one of the topics below. Use the language and ideas that you have learned in this unit. Share your ideas with other students.

Topics:

—leading an adventurous/stable/modern/traditional lifestyle

—making a difficult decision

—someone who taught me about right and wrong

—an experience that made me think about values

—an experience that made me change my mind

—a family member who changed my life

—my favorite memory and what it taught me

—something I want to accomplish in the future

# Unit 3: Wrap Up

**What have you learned about culture shock in this unit? Write your ideas and then tell a classmate. Use these questions to help you:**

What are some things that cause stress in a new culture?

What do you think would make you stressed in a new culture?

How can you try to get over culture shock?

What can happen when you come back to your native country?

What can you learn about yourself by experiencing culture shock?

Do you think you would have a hard time with culture shock? Why or why not?

Have you ever experienced culture shock? If so, how did you get over it?

What advice would you give a person if they just moved to your country?

What is the key to overcoming culture shock?

# Unit 4: Wrap Up

**What are some words in your language that reflect your culture? Write them down, then share them with two classmates.**

Examples:

*Gambatte* means "Do your best." I chose this word because in Japan it is important to always try hard.

*Mei you wen-ti!* means "No problem!" I chose this expression because in China it's important to keep good relations with others.

*Pilseung Korea* means "Victory Korea." I chose this phrase because it became the national cheer for out soccer team during the World Cup, and it shows or pride in our team and in our country.

# Unit 5: Wrap Up

**What customs did you learn about in this unit? Write your answers and give a report to three classmates. Use these questions to help you:**

What body language can cause embarrassment?

What body language can cause people to feel surprised or uncomfortable?

What body language is used to show respect?

What are some customs from Thailand, Saudi Arabia, Malaysia, Egypt, the United States, the Phillippines, Italy, Poland, India, and Greece?

What are four habits that are considered rude in your country?

What are four customs that show respect in your country?

Does kissing mean the same thing in every culture? If not, how does the meaning differ?

What does kissing mean in your country?

# Unit 6: Wrap Up

**Use the ideas that you have learned in this unit to compare the two jobs below. Which company would you like to work for? Why? Share your answers with two classmates.**

*Express Corp.*
Wanted: Free-thinking staff! Work independently and arrange your own schedule. Pay determined by your performance. Call now! 555-4796.

*Interskil Corp.*
Wanted: Friendly, outgoing staff! We have a great team. Join us! Guaranteed salary and training for the right person. Give us a call! 555-8722.

# Unit 7: Wrap Up

**Give advice to a foreign visitor about politeness in your country. Write two things that are polite to do and two things that are impolite to do. Use:**

You should _____.

You should not _____.

Now, share your ideas with two classmates. Did they give the same advice? Discuss.

# Unit 8: Wrap Up

Prepare a short presentation about someone you communicate very well with.
Are there any differences in your communication styles? Explain the differences.

**Possible topics:**

Being expressive helps us to _____.

We're both reserved and it helps us to _____.

My _____ appreciates when I'm subtle.

We express everything. We're very emotional.

Even though I'm calm and he/she's loud, we get along because _____

_____.

We're very honest with each other because _____.

We're both flexible and that helps us to _____.

When we communicate, the most important thing is _____.

# Unit 9: Wrap Up

Choose two opinions from the unit that you agree with, and two that you disagree
with. Write down why you agree or disagree. Include experiences. Use these
questions to help you:

How do different cultures view marriage?

Traditionally, who was expected to have a career in Japan?

Who was expected to raise the kids, cook, and clean?

Are men and women equal nowadays?

Are women better parents than men?

Are men more logical than women?

Who typically disciplines the children in a household?

Who handles the money in the household?

# Unit 10: Wrap Up

**Choose a region from your country to give a presentation about. Use these questions to help you:**

What is special about that region?

What image do other people from your country have about that region?

How do you feel about that region?

Is a different dialect spoken?

What religion is dominant?

Do immigrants live in that region?

What sport is played most in that region?

What is most important to people in that region?

# Unit 11: Wrap Up

**Prepare a short presentation. Choose a famous person who you think has helped your country. Write what you know about his or her life and what he or she did. Present your ideas to a classmate.**

**Possible topics:**

—discrimination and prejudice

—poverty

—social change

—traditional values

—technology

—equal rights

—crime and violence

—equality of the sexes

# Unit 12: Wrap Up

Describe your ideal world. What is it like? Write your ideas, then share them with the class. Use these topics to help you:

—people are different

—people have the same feelings and needs

—having an open mind

—volunteering

—movies

—technology

—salary

—politics

—food

—fashion

—computers

—music

—religion

—sense of right and wrong

—confidence

—intelligence